RESTRUCTURING SOCIETIES

RESTRUCTURING SOCIETIES

Insights from the Social Sciences

Edited by

DAVID B. KNIGHT AND ALUN E. JOSEPH

CARLETON UNIVERSITY PRESS

ISBN 0-88629-350-2 (cloth)
ISBN 0-88629-344-8 (paperback)

Printed and bound in Canada

Canadian Cataloguing in Publication Data

Main entry under title:

Restructuring societies : insights from the social sciences

Based on a series of lectures given by Winegard Visiting
    Professors at the University of Guelph, 1996-97.
Includes bibliographical references and index.
ISBN 0-88629-350-2 (bnd)
ISBN 0-88629-344-8 (pbk)

1. Social policy. 2. Social sciences. I. Knight, David B., 1941
II. Joseph, Alun E., 1950-

H35.R48 1999   300   C98-900915-7

Cover design: Steven Takach
Interior: Lynn's Desktop Publishing

Carleton University Press gratefully acknowledges the support extended to
its publishing program by the Canada Council and the financial assistance
of the Ontario Arts Council. The Press would also like to thank the
Department of Canadian Heritage, Government of Canada, and the
Government of Ontario through the Ministry of Culture, Tourism and
Recreation, for their assistance.

For

The Honourable William Winegard

To the Alma Mater Fund,

Thank you for supporting this series

Bill Winegard

CONTENTS

FIGURES

TABLES

PREFACE

Numerous national societies are undergoing significant economic, social and political "restructuring" as they seek to come to terms with major shifts in the global economy. Statements of this type have become almost truisms, given that so much is being changed rapidly in so many facets of life. The processes of change are many, though much about restructuring and the impact on institutions and, especially, on people is not well understood. Using a variety of social scientific approaches, the authors in this volume consider underlying patterns, processes and consequences associated with restructuring. The volume is intentionally multidisciplinary; the authors themselves are from anthropology, geography, history, Indigenous studies, political studies, psychology, and sociology.

The volume is dedicated to William Winegard, former President of the University of Guelph, who served as a federal Member of Parliament and as Minister for Science and Technology. The University of Guelph's Alma Mater Fund created a continuing Winegard Visiting Professorship in recognition of his remarkable service to the university and to Canada. When the College of Social Science was invited to use the professorship in 1996-97, the decision was made to invite five scholars. In addition to other activities, each of the visitors was invited to give a public lecture addressing a common theme — social sciences and public policy in a restructuring society. Freedom was given to each scholar to approach the theme from the standpoint of their respective disciplines, but with a concern for wider issues and without the use of disciplinary jargon. Perhaps as a consequence of the last two factors, but also because of the rich insights provided by the presenters, the lecture series was a wonderful success. The idea for this book emanated from this series, with four of the lectures being revised for publication and with the addition of two other chapters and an introductory essay. A key issue addressed in this book pertains to the use of words in the discourse on restructuring and the interpretations ascribed to them.

The generous backing of the University of Guelph Alma Mater Fund made this book possible. A significant grant was provided to support the 1996-97 Winegard Visiting Professorship series of lectures and the task of getting this volume published. We are deeply grateful to Olive Dickason, Bob Rae, Julian Barling, Sherwin Rosen and Warren Moran for each spending a week on campus, speaking with students and faculty and delivering public lectures on the topic of this volume. Their willing support, plus that of Jackie Wolfe-Keddie, Belinda Leach and Tony Winson in subsequently providing excellent essays and also generously responding to our editorial demands — and to the suggestions of the anonymous readers selected by Carleton University Press — is most gratefully acknowledged. Regrettably, Sherwin Rosen was unable to provide a written version of his public lecture.

We wish especially to acknowledge the invaluable assistance of Melissa Gabler, without whose remarkable organizational abilities the Winegard Visiting Professorship series would not have functioned as well as it did. Other people deserving special recognition for their roles in helping to bring this book into being include Lynn McDonald, Louis Christofides, Michael Sobol, Maureen Mancuso, Ron Hinch, Michael Matthews, William Christian, Chris McKenna, Marta Rohatynskyj, John Smithers, Carmelina Ridi, Mary Abbott, Reine Oliver, Lois Lindsay, and Marie Puddister, all of whom are at the University of Guelph. From Carleton University or associated with Carleton University Press are Professor Iain Wallace, Dr. John Flood, Jennie Strickland, and Julia Gualtieri, the copy editor, all of whom we also wish to thank.

CONTRIBUTORS

Julian Barling is a Professor of Organizational Behaviour and Psychology in the School of Business at Queen's University in Kingston, Ontario. Born in Rhodesia (now Zimbabwe) and raised and educated in South Africa, he has been in Canada since 1984. A recognized authority on organizational behaviour, his research considers the social, personal and family consequences of economic and organizational change. A prolific contributor to the current journal literature, he has also authored *Employment, Stress and Family Functioning*, co-authored, with C. Fullagar and E. Kevin Kelloway, *The Union and its Members: A Psychological Approach*, and co-edited, with E. Kevin Kelloway, *Young Workers*. He is also co-editor of the book series "Advanced Topics in Organizational Behaviour."

Olive Patricia Dickason is Professor Emerita of History at the University of Alberta and Adjunct Professor at the University of Ottawa. After spending her adolescent and early adult years living on the land in northern Manitoba, she completed her B.A. at Notre Dame College, Wilcox, Saskatchewan, at that time affiliated with the University of Ottawa. She then became an award-winning journalist with newspapers in the prairies, Montreal and Toronto before completing advanced studies at the University of Ottawa. Specializing in Indigenous history, she has published extensively. Her awards include the Canadian Historical Society's Sir John A. Macdonald prize for her groundbreaking *Canada's First Nations: A History of Founding Peoples*, which traces the role of Aboriginal peoples in Canada's story. She is a member of the Order of Canada, was named the 1992 Métis Woman of the Year by the Women of the Métis Nation of Alberta, and holds honorary degrees from several universities, including the University of Guelph.

Alun E. Joseph is Professor of Geography and Chair of the Department of Geography at the University of Guelph. Born and educated in

Wales, he has lived and studied in Canada since 1971. He is a social geographer, with research interests in health-care planning and provision in Canada, New Zealand, and developing countries, and in geographical perspectives on population aging and caregiving to elderly people. In recent research he has focused on the economic and social restructuring of rural communities. He is the author of numerous articles in such journals as *The Canadian Geographer, Canadian Journal on Aging, Journal of Rural Studies, Social Science and Medicine, Progress in Human Geography, Health and Place,* and *Journal of Housing for the Elderly.* He is the co-author, with David R. Phillips, of *Accessibility and Utilization: Geographical Perspectives on Health Care Delivery.*

David B. Knight is Professor of Geography at the University of Guelph, where he served as Dean of the College of Social Science from 1993 to 1998. A cultural and political geographer, he was educated in New Zealand, Scotland and the United States. His Ph.D. is from the University of Chicago. He was the first Chair/Président of the International Geographical Union Commission on the World Political Map (1988 to 1992), and has been a visiting professor at institutions in England, Israel and Russia. He has authored numerous papers in journals and books. His own books include *A Capital for Canada* and *Choosing Canada's Capital: Conflict Resolution in a Parliamentary System.* He edited *Our Geographic Mosaic,* co-edited *Nationalism, Self-Determination and Political Geography* (with Ronald J. Johnston and Eleanore Kofman), and co-authored *Self-Determination* (with Maureen Davies), and *Making Sense in Geography and Environmental Studies* (with Margot Northey).

Belinda Leach is an Assistant Professor of Sociology and Anthropology at the University of Guelph. She received her training as an anthropologist at Carleton University and the University of Toronto and, prior to moving to Guelph in 1993, she taught at McMaster University. Her research focus has been on the impact of restructuring on peoples' lives, in both large urban centres in Canada (such as Hamilton) as well as in rural settings (in areas north of Guelph), and also on informal and domestic work, all with special concern for the role of gender. Her research findings have been published in *The Canadian Review of Sociology and Anthropology, Atlantis, Labour/Le Travail, Critique of Anthropology,* and in books on *Rethinking Restructuring* and *Ethnographic Feminisms.* She is working with Tony Winson on a major research project on economic restructuring and rural community health.

Warren Moran was born and educated in New Zealand and is Professor of Geography at the University of Auckland in New Zealand, where he has also served as Dean of Arts. He is internationally recognized for his work on the restructuring of agriculture, land use competition, and regional processes and policy. He also is an authority on viticulture and he practises sustainable agriculture on his farm in Northland. He has had a long-term leadership role with the international Commission on Changing Rural Systems. He has been a visiting professor at universities in France, the United States, Britain, and Canada. He is First Vice-President of the International Geographical Union. His research is regularly published in such journals as *Environment and Planning, Journal of Rural Studies, New Zealand Geographer,* and *Progress in Human Geography.*

Bob Rae was Premier of the Province of Ontario from 1990 to 1995. He is a member of the Privy Council. Educated at the University of Toronto and Oxford University, where he was a Rhodes Scholar, he subsequently became a lawyer. He entered politics in 1977, winning a seat in 1978 in the federal Parliament for the New Democratic Party. He moved to provincial politics when, in 1982, he became the leader of the Ontario New Democratic Party and then, when the NDP came to power as the Government in 1990, he became Premier. As a politician he was, and he remains, concerned about the dangers of governing in the name of theory, whether of the left or the right. He is now with the law firm of Goodman Phillips and Vineberg in Toronto and lectures at the University of Toronto Law School. He is the author of several books, including his biographical statement entitled, *From Protest to Power: Personal Reflections on a Life in Politics,* and *The Three Questions: Prosperity and the Public Good.*

Anthony Winson is a Professor in the Department of Sociology and Anthropology at the University of Guelph. He received his Ph.D. degree in Sociology from the University of Toronto. He has undertaken research on rural restructuring and job changes in rural communities in Canada, sociological perspectives on agro-food issues, and agrarian social change in Central America. He has served as editor of the newsletter of the Canadian Association for Rural Studies. He has published in such journals as *The Canadian Review of Sociology and Anthropology* and *Rural Sociology,* has authored chapters in several books, and is the author of *The Intimate Commodity: Food and*

Development of the Agro-Industrial Complex in Canada. As noted above, he is a co-researcher with Belinda Leach.

Jackie Wolfe-Keddie is Professor Emerita in the University of Guelph School of Rural Planning and Development. Her continuing scholarly focus is on Indigenous peoples, notably in Canada, with a special interest in how communities can govern themselves and plan for the future. She is the author of numerous publications on these topics including *Sustaining Aboriginal Community Development Planning* and "First Nations' Sovereignty and Land Claims." She is a much-respected speaker nationally and internationally on the challenges faced by Canada's Indigenous peoples.

I

SOCIAL SCIENCES AND PUBLIC POLICY IN RESTRUCTURING SOCIETIES

Alun E. Joseph and David B. Knight

SCOPE, INTENT AND STRUCTURE

IN THIS CHAPTER WE INTRODUCE the theme around which this book is organized and present the topics chosen by our contributors. Our premise is that it is the obligation of the social sciences to comment critically on the origins, mechanisms and impacts of restructuring, with the latter broadly conceived as rapid and far-reaching economic and social change amounting to a "changing of the rules" under which people experience society. In particular, we see social science commentaries as important to an enhanced understanding of restructuring outcomes, especially as they affect real people living in specific places as opposed to depersonalized and placeless producers and consumers. We ascribe to the view that such an appreciation of the "situated meaning"of restructuring is a prerequisite for informed debate on the (re)formulation of public policy.

The ways in which individual social scientists have contributed to an understanding of the situated meaning of restructuring have been influenced considerably by their disciplinary affiliations and theoretical perspectives. However, we do not attempt to classify themes and approaches by discipline or school of thought; neither do we seek to attach value to particular areas of scholarship, thus elevating the work of some over that by others. Instead, we promote the value of diversity, in research topics and in ways of conducting research, as a means of building a broad base for public policy formation. This said, we must acknowledge that while we endeavour in this chapter to provide a broad review of subject matter and approaches, our arguments spring very much from our disciplinary roots in human geography and draw substantively upon our individual research experiences. The subsequent chapters approach our theme of "social sciences and public policy in restructuring societies" from perspectives that draw upon the disciplinary origins of the authors — geography, history, political studies, psychology, sociology, anthropology, and Indigenous studies — and reflect their substantive interests.

The remainder of this chapter is organized in four major sections. The first of these briefly outlines a geopolitical context. The second deconstructs the theme to build, sequentially, an appreciation of restructuring, of public policy in restructuring societies, and of the role of social sciences in critiquing and informing such policy. The third section moves away from these more abstract, theoretical debates to consider some selected studies of the restructuring of health services. The health sector is chosen as the focus for a discussion of the situated meaning of restructuring because of its centrality to the modern welfare state. Case studies from New Zealand, a country often held up as a model of a restructured society (Kelsey, 1997), are deliberately juxtaposed with a consideration of parallel initiatives in Canada. The fourth and final section introduces the topics addressed by our contributors, noting linkages among them and with the themes introduced in this chapter.

THE CHANGING GEOPOLITICAL CONTEXT

The world's political map has undergone major restructuring since World War II. The first major sweep of changes occurred in the 1950s and 1960s as the decolonization process unfolded rapidly with remarkable consequences. "Modernization" emerged quickly as the principal ideology driving change. Societies were altered in accordance with the belief that "traditional" ways of life had to be replaced with modern (Western) notions of industrialization, education and health standards. Social scientists studied the pace of social change and also the conditions under which change occurred. They noted that modernization sometimes engendered a politics of resistance (Eisenstadt, 1966) and, despite certain expectations (Rostow, 1960; Hoffman, 1962), did not always lead to the expected outcome of sustained economic growth through industrialization.

Other changes to the world political map resulted from secessionist forms of self-determination, including the formation of Bangladesh from part of Pakistan, and, more recently, Eritrea from part of Ethiopia. The move to greater autonomy for Scotland and less so for Wales under the policy of devolution adopted by the British Labour

Government elected in 1997 suggests that the search for solutions to problems of identity-territory "fit" is far from being a spent process. Indeed, a second sweep of major politico-territorial changes resulting from the failure of state communism and the collapse of the Soviet state can be viewed as both a form of decolonization and as a search for "better" definitions of society. Secessionist states such as Lithuania and Ukraine claimed self-determination and became independent. In the same time period, many former Soviet "satellites" such as Poland and Hungary experienced internal self-determination as existing governments were thrown out and replaced by new governments, with fundamental alterations being made in response to reformed societal expectations (O'Loughlin and van der Wusten, 1993). Just as the processes and outcomes of the collapse of state communism have overlapped with those of decolonization, in the late twentieth century the attribution of cause and effect in societal change has become even more problematic as a consequence of a third sweep of changes resulting from globalization.

Globalization refers to the increasing sway of a new form of capitalism characterized by the increased mobility of capital and the rise of transnational corporations, facilitated by the rapid evolution of worldwide digital communications technology (Thrift, 1995). As Thrift and others have observed, "the new system of capitalism attacks and suppresses distance, *and* our notions of distance, producing a new global economic space in which global capitalism can play" (Thrift, 1995, 19-20). In a broader sense, globalization also describes important qualitative changes in realms other than the economic; it describes a suite of orchestrated changes in the cultural, political, social and environmental realms (Taylor, Watts and Johnston, 1995). It can be argued that such changes are "revolutionary" because they are, in Jameson's (1991, xxi) words, "more thoroughgoing and all-pervasive" than the previous period of modernization and industrialization.

Globalization presents a challenge to states for economic, political and cultural processes have increasingly cut across state borders and undercut their significance as arbitrars of world order. In the era of *internationalization* that dominated most of this century, the state was pre-eminent: world trade was an extension of *economic* activity across national borders; *cultural* exchanges were centred on national institutions; and the state itself was the pre-eminent agent and site of *political change* (Le Heron and Pawson, 1996). Globalization heralds the advent of new times in which state-centred human activities are fading in importance (Taylor, Watts and Johnston, 1995). The state still holds importance as a locus for regulation, but the parameters of national policy formulation are increasingly constrained by forces that are supranational.

It is very easy to exaggerate the importance of globalization (Thrift, 1995), and there is no single path along which states are being forced or led (James and Jackson, 1993). However, in many countries, including New Zealand, Great Britain and Canada, restructuring has seemed to flow inexorably from the individual and collective efforts of political and economic leaders to effect change at the local level as they seek to adapt to a changing world economy. Historically contingent patterns of regulation are increasingly being challenged by new regimes of production, exchange and consumption. These new ways of doing things demand a rethinking of the relationships between scales of activity, of the role of democratic institutions forged in a previous era of modernization and internationalization, and of commitments to the collective provision of goods and services. To take us back nearly to where we started, restructuring, and especially the change in state regulatory capacity, carries with it the potential for nationalistic demands for enhanced rights of citizenship, even to the point of challenges being made to state structures.

Demands for enhanced rights are becoming more evident in many places. For instance, Québécois nationalists desire separation from Canada as a way of ensuring their place in the new global order. However, in contrast, Aboriginal people in Canada, including those within Québec, insist that their rights to territory and associated claims to autonomy must be considered as pre-eminent within the Canadian constitutional debate (Grand Council of the Crees, 1998; Jensen, 1995; Knight, 1988, 1998a). In these conflicts we see the apparent paradox of increased nationalism at a time of growing globalization. The tension between nationalism (and other forms of group self-definition) and globalization might well constitute a major driving force that could soon lead to a further sweep of changes to the world's political map because at base level there remains a tension: should primacy be given to territory and, secondarily, the people within it, or to peoples and, secondarily, the territories they inhabit (Knight, 1982, 1985)? Currently, in the state-structured world, primacy is given to state territories which, it is held, define the "people" (Knight, 1995). But globalization is leading to a *decrease* in importance of territory as defined by the international system of states. This reality is gradually undercutting national identities as we know them today. If the significance of states continues to be weakened economically, it seems almost inevitable that the current primacy given to national identities as defined by states in terms of concepts like citizenship will also be weakened. Consequently, groups of people may well seek new definitions of identity. While some such future group identities may not be territorially bound, there is evidence to suggest that new group politico-territorial identities will be created (Knight, 1995), which necessarily will result in changes to the world's political map.

The possible restructuring of the world map as a consequence of globalization is now being explored from a variety of perspectives, not least of which is a concern for the changing location and importance of political boundaries and communities' conceptualizations of their territories (Paasi, 1995; Garrick, 1998), with due regard for the linked importance of geography and history as attempts are made to understand what it means to be modern (Taylor, 1999). Such investigations represent the geopolitical backdrop for the essays in this volume, which are concerned with situated processes and effects of change; our contributors deal with the locally or nationally manifested form, style and various impacts of restructuring. From this brief overview of the geopolitical context, we now turn to focusing on the theme of the book.

DECONSTRUCTING THE THEME

"If there is a word for every season it is 'restructuring.'"
(Britton, *et al.*, 1992, 2)

The term "restructuring" was first used in the mid-1970s to describe the "once-only" measures taken by industries to adjust to changing global trade conditions after the end of the "long boom" that followed the World War II (Le Heron and Pawson, 1996). As such, the term denoted an acceleration of processes of adjustment that are endemic in capitalist societies, and, as noted in the previous section, it is important not to lose sight of the historical continuity and contingency of events. Not only were marked changes in modes of production in the 1970s part of a continuous process of adjustment by enterprises to shifting currents of competition, they were also historically contingent on the cumulative effects of previous adjustments. The preoccupation with the sphere of production in early commentaries about restructuring led writers such as Sayer (1985) to advocate a broader interpretation of the term to embrace changes in the rapidly expanding service sector. In the context of public services, restructuring is generally taken to describe an orchestrated set of policy measures and institutional actions aimed at reducing commitments to the welfare state (Pinch, 1989).

In several countries, in the mid-1980s, there was a broadening of the academic discourse on restructuring away from its industrial, private-sector origins. This was coincidental with a questioning of the role of state as a producer of goods and services and as a regulator of private spheres of production and consumption. In New Zealand, for instance, it was argued that "the economy was riddled with interventions introduced to mitigate unfortunate side-effects of earlier interventions. In turn, they required further interventions to deal with their side-effects" (Easton, 1997, 7). This dissatisfaction with the regulatory status quo provided the platform for the "New Zealand experiment," in which "successive governments applied pure economic theory to a complex, real life community, with generally cavalier disregard for the social or electoral consequences" (Kelsey, 1997, 1). The neo-liberal ideology underlying restructuring became evident in the frequent calls "to restore competitiveness," to "reintroduce the free market" and to "give investors greater autonomy" (Le Heron and Pawson, 1996, 5). Consequently, discussions of restructuring have grown beyond the consideration of "once-only" changes in industrial organization to describe a large-scale *political* agenda for societal change that transcends its economic and largely theoretical origins.

As studies of restructuring have accumulated, it has become increasingly evident that the effects of restructuring can never be wholly contained, either sectorally or geographically. It is virtually impossible to insulate one sector of society or sphere of government activity from the direct or indirect impacts of restructuring in other sectors or spheres, even if this is deemed to be desirable. Neither is it possible to shield specific regions or localities from restructuring effects (Britton, et al., 1992). Thus, discussions of public policy on restructuring now encompass not only a consideration of its economic and political origins, beginning from the premise "that 'restructuring' springs from the deliberate, calculated and creative acts of people" (Britton, et al., 1992, 2), but also encompass the various outcomes of restructuring, considered either individually or in aggregate. These outcomes are inscribed on the social and economic fabric of communities in particular places (Massey, 1991) and in the lives of individuals

(Kearns and Joseph, 1997); they are manifested in the opening of opportunities for some and the closing of opportunities for others.

As geographers, we are very sensitive to "place," and its sociological analogue, "community," as the location in which and from which people experience a restructuring society (Agnew, 1987; Keith and Pile, 1993; Wallace and Knight, 1996). Almost paradoxically, as globalization has reduced spatial barriers and shortened time horizons, thereby enhancing possibilities for more immediate and intensive interaction between hitherto distant places (Allen and Hamnett, 1995; *Geographical Review*, 1997), places and their communities have, in another sense, become more differentiated. Capital, operating at scales from the local to the international, has sought to exploit the particular characteristics of places, thereby promoting uneven development (Massey and Jess, 1995). However, we are also cognizant of other themes in other disciplines which constitute equally valid "windows" on the nature of restructuring and its implications for public policy. Several of these have already been noted, and they and others feature in the various contributions to this book. Additional themes, not yet mentioned but given considerable attention in the Canadian literature, include the impacts of restructuring on organized labour (Pupo and White, 1994) and on women (Macdonald, 1995). The intersection of these two themes, at which questions are asked about how an expanding cohort of women has fared in union workplaces exposed to restructuring (Brisken, 1994; Creese, 1995), is particularly interesting because it foreshadows an important argument in the following section: restructuring modifies, and is modified by, other social processes, in this case, the feminization of the workforce.

The broadening of the academic discourse on restructuring has been accompanied by a widening of the theoretical perspectives brought to bear on restructuring issues by social scientists. While varying across disciplines and depending to some degree on whether or not the focus has predominantly been upon the causes, mechanisms or outcomes of restructuring, there has generally been a move away from the narrowly focused political-economy approaches characteristic of early analyses to encompass more humanistic and idiosyncratic narratives. This broadening of perspectives has been encouraged, at least in some instances, by the post-modern challenge to make room for "difference"and "otherness" in social science (Kearns and Joseph, 1997).

In terms of a critical analysis of the impact of restructuring on the welfare state, which is considered in more detail in the following sec-

tion, Pinch (1997) notes progress in the development of transdiscipli-
nary theory in three areas: Regulation Theory, Structuration Theory
and the "Cultural Turn." Regulation theory, which springs from the
Marxist approach in political economy, views the differential responses of nation-states to globalization in terms of changes in the complex
systems of regulation affecting the spheres of economic and social organization. As such, regulation theory is most suited to an analysis of
broad changes in national welfare regimes (Pinch, 1997). Of particular
significance is the recent shift in focus to "real regulation," where interest is transferred from the consideration of policy development to a
scrutiny of how policy is implemented through administrative practices
and procedures (Clark, 1992). Such an approach is, in many senses,
a fundamental building block for a critical analysis of restructuring.
What is often painted as *de*regulation is often *re*regulation to achieve
particular, largely ideological goals (Kelsey, 1997).

Regulation theory is not very amenable to application at regional
and local levels (Pinch, 1997). At such levels, structuration theory
(Giddens, 1984; 1991) provides a means of bridging the gap between
an appreciation of restructuring as a process of change and the lives of
people who experience the impacts of such change. Structuration theory is a form of contextual analysis that seeks to find a middle ground
intellectually between studies of societal structures and analyses of
human behaviour. While most approaches in social science almost
invariably recognize the importance of both "structure" and "human
agency," narratives of change almost as certainly concentrate upon one
direction of causality. Many studies of economic change, for instance,
pay only lip-service to understanding changes made by people.
Conversely, many studies of individual adaptation tend to look at the
surrounding environment merely as some sort of static backcloth
(Pinch, 1997, 96). Structuration theory contends that social systems
are created cumulatively through human action and serve to condition
and constrain such action. In studies of the restructuring of the welfare
state, structuration theory points to the possibility for human agency,
which in turn creates the potential for structural changes to have variable impacts on communities and their residents.

The "cultural turn" in social science represents the third and,
arguably, most important, of the three threads of theory development
noted by Pinch (1997). Its importance is twofold. First, cultural studies has refocused attention on power, and in this sense links can be
drawn to regulation theory. Restructuring can be viewed as an ideolog-

ical project, with control of the language of restructuring as a key weapon in the arsenal of change. The power to impose language and attendant meaning on the discourse of restructuring brings with it possibilities for control (Kelsey, 1997). Second, cultural studies has encouraged a broader analysis of restructuring, in which the entanglement, one with another, of short-term changes in civil society are considered alongside longstanding issues such as racism and the systematic marginalization of women in the workforce. This is not to say, of course, that all studies of race and welfare or the feminist critique of restructuring can be classified under the banner of cultural studies. The key is a shared valuing of critical assessment as a prerequisite for debate on public policy.

Regardless of discipline and perspective, engagement with restructuring has been a defining experience for many social scientists, in the sense that social constructions of restructuring, expressed in the words of politicians, public servants and the general public, not only shape lay discourse on restructuring but also influence restructuring as a *political* process. Meanings attached to terms like rightsizing, re-engineering, downsizing, rationalizing, reorganizing, realignment and reform are consistently being formed and (re)formed through dialogue and debate. Consequently, we reiterate the point that social scientists must strive to attain a *situated* meaning for restructuring (Kearns and Joseph, 1997), for as Pinch (1989, 905) notes, the concept has obtained "a high level of use and a low level of meaning."

RESTRUCTURING HEALTH CARE:
BUILDING HEALTHY MINDS AND HEALTHY BODIES?

To deepen the understanding of restructuring processes and outcomes it is useful to consider examples of restructuring in the health sector. The examples focus on the restructuring of secondary and tertiary care, which is almost always a euphemism for the closure of hospitals. Research by Alun Joseph and colleagues in New Zealand is used as the initial, empirical platform for discussion, and links are made with some current developments in Ontario. Rural circumstances and developments are emphasized, and the theoretical perspectives (regulation theory, structuration theory and cultural studies) outlined earlier are used as a loose framework:
• to make transparent the ideological aspects of restructuring;
• to outline the complex and pervasive effects of single-sector

restructuring initiatives on the economic viability and social
vitality of communities and on the sustainability of people's
lives; and

•   to demonstrate the historical and geographical contingency of
restructuring effects.

Health care systems are hierarchies, usually generalized into three
levels: primary care based on general practitioners and other "front
line" providers (but also including family and self-care); secondary care
based on general hospitals; and tertiary care centred in specialized hospitals (Joseph and Phillips, 1984). Restructuring of health care can
involve the re-allocation of responsibility either within a particular level
of the health care hierarchy or between levels, or both. Our emphasis
here is on hospital-based care at the secondary and tertiary levels, and
our central proposition is that the proponents of restructuring consistently ignore the broader meanings of change for affected communities
and underestimate the potential for human agency.

Health care lies at the heart of the welfare state, such that even the
most enthusiastic proponents of restructuring have found it a "difficult
nut to crack." In New Zealand, for instance, health care remained relatively untouched by a reform-minded Labour government (1984-90).
While the rhetoric of reform spoke to the need to *target* public-sector
health services at those with both high need and limited ability to pay,
to *rationalize* services to yield better economic of scale, and to *privatize*
selected responsibilities in the health sector (Kearns and Barnett, 1992;
Joseph and Chalmers, 1995), the health sector remained virgin territory for the restructuring zeal of the more conservative, National government that came to power in 1990 (Easton, 1997; Kelsey, 1997). In
1993, the National government introduced market forces into the
state-funded health sector. Government-appointed regional health
authorities (RHAs) would purchase care from providers, which included
clusters of commercially-driven public hospitals (known as Crown
Health Enterprises) and a range of private and voluntary providers
(Blank, 1994; Malcolm and Barnett, 1994).

Changes in the quantity and character of health care has been one
of the defining features of structural change affecting New Zealand's
urban and rural communities in the 1990s, but rural communities have
felt the impact of health-sector restructuring most acutely. *Ration-
alization* of state-funded health care services has translated into the
closure of small rural hospitals (Le Heron and Pawson, 1996). The
concomitant (but by no means consistent) expansion of services in

larger (urban) hospitals has proven to be of problematic benefit to many of those in *targeted* groups (the elderly, Maori, the unemployed) because public transportation services have declined dramatically in rural areas (O'Hare, 1994). For example, in their analysis of population-aging dynamics and long-term care provision in the Waikato region, Joseph and Chalmers (1995; 1996) found that in the late 1980s the long-term care system expanded considerably faster than did the numbers of elderly people in the region. However, substantial financial and distance barriers discouraged use of new private, *urban* facilities by the rural elderly. The latter appeared to be staying on in increasing numbers in service-depleted villages and small towns. *Privatization* has not brought new services into small rural communities for the same reason that underlay the collapse of collective (state) provision. Dispersed populations in rural areas rarely, if ever, meet the critical demand thresholds for the efficient (read profitable) provision of health services (Kearns and Joseph, 1997).

As noted earlier, studies of particular restructuring initiatives are the building blocks for identifying the situated meaning of restructuring. A study by Joseph and Kearns (1996) of the closure of Tokanui Hospital, one of the four major facilities serving the needs of mentally ill and intellectually disabled people in the North Island of New Zealand, provides an illustration of the interconnection of a restructuring initiative with other processes of social significance, in this case, the deinstitutionalization of mental health care services and the assertion of Maori identity and rights.

On April 29, 1993, 600 full- and part-time workers, many of whom were Maori, were told of the intent to close the 80-year-old institution in June 1995. Tokanui Hospital, it was announced, would be replaced by a psychiatric care centre on the grounds of the Waikato Hospital in Hamilton and by a network of community housing for the intellectually disabled. Joseph and Kearns (1996) suggest that while the closure of Tokanui Hospital can be seen as another step in the de-institutionalization of mental health care, it also presents itself as an example of public sector restructuring, whereby jobs are removed from a rural region with few alternative employment opportunities and relocated to an urban centre 35 km away, already well endowed with services and attendant job opportunities. In addition to the employment factor, Joseph and Kearns note the loss of symbolic identity for the rural community around Tokanui and the dismantling of important and nationally applauded Maori initiatives in mental health care. They

conclude that in the Tokanui case, "the *philosophy* of deinstitutionalization has been effectively captured by the *ideology* of restructuring"
(Joseph and Kearns, 1996, 187). While arguments for deinstitutionalization fuelled professional and public compliance with closure of a
custodial institution, the proponents of restructuring have not taken up
the community care option with any great enthusiasm; indeed, a delay
in the closure of Tokanui Hospital was announced in mid-1995
because funding arrangements for replacement services could not be
settled (Kearns and Joseph, 1997).

Kearns and Joseph (1997) compare the events surrounding the
announced closure of Tokanui Hospital with those associated with
attempts to dismantle the Hokianga Special Medical Area (SMA). The
Hokianga is a remote locality surrounding a harbour of the same name
in the Northland Region. It is an economically poor region with one of
the highest unemployment rates in New Zealand. A majority of the
region's population identify themselves as Maori (Kearns and Reinken,
1994). Owing to its remoteness and poor economic base, the Hokianga
was designated as New Zealand's first SMA in 1947. A key benefit of
this status was that primary and secondary health care (including prescriptions) was provided free of charge to all local residents regardless
of their individual financial circumstances (Kearns, 1991).

In 1991, a proposal to abolish free prescriptions was seen by local
residents as a precursor of a complete dissolution of the SMA, and pre-
cipitated a highly spatialized politics of resistance. Community opposition was initially articulated through a threatened *hikoi tapu* (holy
walk) to the Parliament in Wellington by both Maori and Pakeha
(New Zealanders of European extraction) residents. In December
1991, a community committee successfully negotiated with the
Minister of Health to institute a pilot program in which the Hokianga
Health Enterprises Trust (HHET) would hold a budget for the region's
total pharmaceutical costs. The resolve of the HHET to maintain free
health care in the Hokianga was hardened in 1992 when charges for
public hospital care were instituted nationally. Late in 1992, the HHET
sought assurances from Northland Health Ltd. (the local CHE) that
existing services would remain in Hokianga, and that the long-standing absence of charges would persist. No such guarantee was forthcoming, so the HHET campaigned to take over all responsibility for
health care in the Hokianga. With support from the local *purchaser* of
services (North Health), and despite opposition from the local *provider*
of health care (Northland Health Ltd.), the HHET was successful. On

July 1, 1992, the Associate Minister of Health handed over all the health care assets in the Hokianga to the chairperson of the trust, a local Maori elder (Kearns and Joseph, 1997).

The two narratives presented above indicate two divergent community outcomes of health care restructuring. In the Tokanui case, the closure of the hospital represents a closing of opportunities — for employment, for the promotion of symbolic identity, and for the assertion of Maori identity. In contrast, in the Hokianga, the threat to disestablish the Hokianga SMA resulted in the opening of opportunities for enhanced community participation in, and control of, health care delivery. Examination of the two cases through the three "lenses" of regulation theory, structuration theory and cultural studies, suggests critical differences between them.

In the Tokanui case, a process of reregulation of health care whereby services were to be re-sited to a highly institutionalized medical complex in Hamilton, was obfuscated by an emphasis in discourse on the closure of a custodial institution. Concerns with loss of employment and broader implications for the community were set against the advantages to patients of relocation. Indeed, the almost total lack of human agency in the Tokanui case, the virtual absence of any organized resistance, can perhaps be attributed to the fact that liberal-minded community leaders sympathized with the idea of closing an institution "replete with connotations of outdated treatment modalities" (Kearns and Joseph, 1997, 28). In the Hokianga case, the attempts to reregulate local health services were immediately recognized as a direct threat to the health of residents and to the survival of the local community. Local leadership quickly emerged to seek a local solution to what was perceived as the imposition of an ill-fitting national model of health care delivery. Agency was asserted through aggressive disputation of the language of restructuring. The transformation of public hospitals into Crown Health Enterprises, mandated to turn a profit, was portrayed as a key component of reregulation. Simultaneously, the recasting of the public as consumers was resisted.

Lest it be thought that these New Zealand examples are novel, we will conclude this discussion of health care restructuring by referring to a debate, one amongst many currently, about hospital restructuring (i.e., closure) in Ontario. This debate is province-wide and features a commission (The Health Services Restructuring Commission) which travels across the province, deciding in a matter of weeks the fate of local and regional systems of secondary and tertiary care that have taken decades to evolve. In keeping with the rural emphasis identified above, the example chosen is Chesley which lies within the jurisdiction of the Grey-Bruce District Health Council (DHC). Like other planning regions, the Grey-Bruce DHC has been charged with developing a restructuring plan for hospitals that will reduce the aggregate base budget by 18 percent over three years.

The 20-bed Chesley and District Memorial Hospital is a survivor of previous restructuring exercises. The hospital was ordered closed in 1976, reprieved after a community outcry, and rebuilt in 1982 with provincial government support matching local fund-raising (*Sun Times*, October 11, 1996). A report tabled by the DHC on February 4, 1997 proposed closing the hospital's twenty beds and downgrading the facility to a primary health centre (*Sun Times*, February 5, 1997). The community responded to the announcement with a St. Valentine's Day public protest involving close to half the town's 1900 citizens. As one participant put it, "we pay taxes just the same as anybody else. We have the right to have our local hospital" (*Sun Times*, February 15, 1997). Some commentators deplored the way that the restructuring proposal was pitting community against community. Others pointed out the special problems of less mobile residents, such as the elderly and members of the local Old Order Mennonite community (*Sun Times*, February 21, 1997).

An examination of planning documents and media reports indicates significant divergence in the conceptualization of the issue at hand: the DHC and its consultants expressed the proposals for restructuring the Grey-Bruce hospital system in terms of cost-effectiveness (albeit in pursuit of the provincial government's slippery notion of "the best service at the least cost"), while the public in communities like Chesley interpreted proposals as a threat to their communities. Thus, one discourse speaks objectively about bed numbers and hospital budgets, and another speaks subjectively about the impact on people's lives and the symbolic identity of communities. Each side is then bemused by the lack of understanding on the part of the other. An interesting twist in the debate about the Grey-Bruce hospitals is the expression of agency through the generation of an alternative restructuring plan by an "alliance" of four hospitals (including Chesley) that would generate marginally more savings across the four than would the DHC proposal, save more then 50 percent on capital redevelopment costs, and keep all four facilities as hospitals (*Sun Times*, February 15, 1997). As the alliance spokesperson put it, "this is not someone from Toronto telling us how our services should be run.... No solution could be more local than this" (*Sun Times*, February 15, 1997). Notwithstanding this assertion, it will be the Health Service Restructuring Commission that will decide the fate of the Chesley Hospital. Fittingly, then, we can close our discussion of health care restructuring by repeating our assertion that such processes are, above all, political ones through which the rules under which people experience society are changed.

The search for a situated meaning for restructuring will continue in the coming years. The pace of structural change continues to be rapid and widespread, such that changes in one sector modify, and are modified by, changes in other sectors, with effects crossing and recrossing scales from the individual to the state itself. We join with others in arguing that public policy needs to be based less on ideology and more on the results of debate in which proposals are fully contextualized and potential consequences freely acknowledged. Claims of success will continue to warrant particular attention. For instance, perverse claims of success in health care restructuring based upon the number of dollars saved (through closing hospitals or reducing services) need to be matched against achievements in improving health. Neo-liberal proponents of restructuring will continue to brand critique by stakeholders as "lobbying by interest groups" and to vaunt the success of restructuring internationally. However, such claims often fail to survive close scrutiny. For instance, New Zealanders, who collectively underwent a period of unprecedented postwar economic and social upheaval between 1985 and 1992, saw their economy shrink by one percent compared to an OECD average growth of 20 percent in the same time period (Kelsey, 1997, 9). The legacy in that country of a headlong rush to restructuring, largely uninformed by public policy debate, has been a massive social, cultural and democratic deficit (Kelsey, 1997).

THE CONTRIBUTORS AND THE IMPORTANCE OF WORDS

With the above thoughts as guidance, we now consider the remaining contributions to this book. The contributors address the theme of social science and public policy in restructuring societies in their own distinctive ways, echoing the diversity of understanding of restructuring and of its interrelationship with public policy as noted earlier.

Bob Rae focuses on the role of ideology as a raison d'être for revolutionary change. Drawing from the works of 18th century political theorist and parliamentarian, Edmund Burke, and 20th century author

George Orwell, he develops an argument for the pre-eminence of fact over theory and reason over revolution in government. Citizens, he argues, should be sceptical of any regime that governs in the name of revolution, be it of the left or the right. The significance of Rae's comments should not be taken lightly (see Rae, 1996). As the former New Democratic Party Premier of the Province of Ontario, he has seen the hasty dismantlement by the successor Progressive Conservative Government of numerous government programs that had taken decades to develop. The Conservative Government is taking, in Rae's words, "libertarian excesses" as it relentlessly pursues its goals as part of, in the government's own words, "the common sense revolution." Burke and Orwell surely would have had a field day writing about Ontario's current ideologically based "revolution."

Warren Moran also takes up the theme of ideology. He presents the radical restructuring of New Zealand society in the decade following 1984 — a year of Orwellian significance! He views restructuring as an orchestrated political and bureaucratic project driven by neo-liberal ideology. This project, manifested in a reregulation of economy and society that reasserted the authority of central government over the local state, was legitimated by untried economic theory, with little of the empirical validation called for by Bob Rae. Moran notes that the project was championed by a few key politicians and institutions. In the process of pursuing what was presented as the only solution to New Zealand's external debt problem, these key players eschewed social democratic principles and subverted institutions and practices of social democracy. As noted earlier, the anticipated and much unanticipated impact of economic reform penetrated to every corner of New Zealand. The parallel with what has been happening in Ontario is striking for there, too, personal wisdom and decision making has been elevated over public debate and consensus seeking.

The contributions by Julian Barling and by Belinda Leach and Tony Winson shift our attention to the workplace, where major changes are occurring as a result of restructuring in the private and public sectors. The changing organization of production is central to Barling's analysis of employment relations in the restructured workplaces of contemporary Canada. He argues that while change is endemic to organizations, the amount, nature and pace of change currently confronting both employers and employees is unprecedented. A "job for a lifetime" is now a rare thing. Similarly, loyalty to a single employer has waned. Practices such as outsourcing have served to institutionalize an age of specialization and constant innovation in which employees are offered "contingent jobs" for short periods of time, with time-limited contracts holding pre-eminence over careers. These changes have profound implications for the relationship between work and family life and for the sustainability of the social institutions of work. Barling suggests that employers, unions and government regulators need to redefine their roles in this new world of work.

Leach and Winson provide a local, situated view of change in the world of work by considering the impact of plant closures in three small towns on the lives of displaced workers. They point out the tensions between, on the one hand, the rosy view of community futures promoted by local politicians intent on attracting "footloose" industries, and on the other, the lived experience of the local casualties of globalization. Local politicians attempt to remain positive and "boosterist" in an effort not to scare off potential employers who may move into their towns. At the same time, displaced workers bemoan the loss of well-paid, unionized jobs. Leach and Winson make very real the notion, foreshadowed by us earlier with reference to the work of Kearns and Joseph (1997), that restructuring is recorded on the economic and social fabric of communities and inscribed in the lives of people. Their concern for the impact of restructuring on peoples' lives is important, for despite globalization processes being far distant in origin and generally difficult to fully comprehend, the local remains the focus for peoples' everyday living. It is thus important to remember that "the local will always matter, no matter what is happening at the global scale" (Knight, 1998b, 149).

Changes to regulation, either embedded in legislation or enshrined in administrative practice, are essential to restructuring. Rae and Moran identify how individuals and small groups can decide to effect change according to an ideology and, by control of key political and economic institutions, can implement necessary changes. Olive Dickason, in her review of the role and importance of treaties for Aboriginal societies, and Jackie Wolfe-Keddie in her discussion of the restructuring of the relationship between Aboriginal peoples and the Canadian state, come at the issue of regulation from different perspectives.

Dickason argues strongly for the historical contingency of what appear to be contemporary issues. She demonstrates that the meaning of treaties for Aboriginal societies, in the past and as they affect present disputes over land and resources, is shaped by Aboriginal understanding of natural law as the basis for agreements. Such an understanding did not, and still does not, fit well with the highly situated, legalistic interpretations of British colonial authorities and, later, with governments in the successor Canadian state. The increasing likelihood that the rights of Aboriginal peoples under natural law will be recognized in future land claims and self-governance settlements will undoubtedly influence the way that restructuring processes will, in turn, affect Aboriginal peoples. This conclusion is supported by the identification by Kearns and Joseph (1997) of biculturalism as an important modifier of restructuring outcomes. This stated, Canada's governments have not always been respectful of cultural differences. Further, and here we reflect on the importance of Dickason's chapter, Canada — as institution and as dominant society — has not always been observant of treaty rights with its First Nations. Indeed, using words carefully, Canada and its federal and provincial governments have neither treated the Aboriginal peoples as equals — as implied in the treaties — or generously (Dickason, 1994).

Given that Canada and Canadians generally are experiencing remarkable changes as a consequence of restructuring, it has become critical for the dominant society (and its national and provincial governments) to relate to the Aboriginal peoples in new ways. A change of attitude on the part of the dominant society is needed since Canada's Aboriginal peoples are demanding the self-determination and self-control which they maintain are essential to cultural survival. Interestingly, restructuring in New Zealand offers Canadians a compelling lesson, as noted by Moran. He clearly supports Dickason's contention that treaties are of critical importance. He also notes that the very government that has been dismantling the welfare state in New Zealand has moved quickly to resolve long-standing Maori land and resource ownership and autonomy issues — with due regard for treaties. Seemingly, the recent commitment to full-scale restructuring created a willingness and the wherewithal (through asset sales) on the part of the Government of New Zealand to deal with Aboriginal (Maori) issues that had seemingly been beyond the capacity of previous administrations. Will the same hold true in Canada? Wolfe-Keddie is not wildly optimistic as she explores the wide-ranging changes that have been effected and the further changes that are being called for in Canada. It remains to be seen whether a similar willingness and capacity for settling Aboriginal issues to that found recently in New Zealand will emerge in the provinces of Alberta and Ontario, positioned as they are at the vanguard of restructuring within Canada. If this does happen, then the Aboriginal peoples in Canada, as with Maoris in New Zealand, will themselves become important agents of change, for they will have the confidence and wherewithal to restructure their own lives and communities.

Wolfe-Keddie identifies an essential challenge to the liberal democracy notion of all people being equal and that they should be treated equally when she observes that "Aboriginal people insist they are 'citizens different,' and have legal, constitutional and historical evidence, and moral argument, to support their claim." Acceptance of this reality by the dominant society would form "the foundation stone" for renewed relationships and meaningful restructuring, but, she notes, up to now "there has been no sustained, constructive and willing engagement of non-Aboriginal Canadian society to implement the vision of a joint and mutually respectful project of reconciliation, restructuring and reconstruction."

Wolfe-Keddie gives special attention to the use of words. In considering words that Indigenous peoples have used as they have sought to place themselves in a context apart from the dominant society in Canada, Wolfe-Keddie highlights a theme implicit in *all* of the chapters, namely, that the very structure of knowledge has changed as people and their institutions have had to come to terms with the processes and consequences of restructuring. For instance, universities, schools and school boards, unions, hospitals, businesses, government at all levels, newspapers, and so on, are all having to contend with changing words, conceptualizations, and expectations, not just changing structures. Since restructuring is so pervasive, and invasive, the very word restructuring is taken to mean different things by different people depending, in part, on their position and orientation, such as politician (in power or not), banker, corporate leader, union boss, employed or unemployed worker, and so on.

Earlier in this chapter we noted that meanings attached to terms like rightsizing, downsizing, etc., have consistently been formed and (re)formed through dialogue and debate. The issue for social scientists — and for all others in society — is to attain a *situated* meaning for restructuring so we can, in time, go beyond Pinch's (1989, 905) observation that restructuring has obtained "a high level of use and a low level of meaning." Pinch is correct: the term has indeed attained widespread use yet it is not always clear what is meant by the term. This reality is illustrated effectively by the authors within this book who, from a diversity of social science disciplinary approaches and theoretical orientations, draw valuable insights as a result of being focussed on a common theme.

We believe that the reader of the essays in this volume will gain a strength of understanding from the variety of disciplinary concerns and analytical scales adopted by our contributors. While there is a diversity of views and contrasting insights, there is also commonality: each author is concerned with the impact of purposeful societal change. The approach to change is through application of substantive interpretive frameworks — regarding changing interpretations of political theory in a revolutionary context (Rae), the changing role of expectations for Indigenous peoples in relation to the British colonial and the successor Canadian state (Dickason, Wolfe-Keddie), or the role of selected people and institutions (Moran) — through interpretive analysis of data that provides critical insight into how restructuring is fundamentally altering societies — in Canada (Barling, Leach and Winson) and New Zealand (Moran, and us in this chapter) — and through a humanistic consideration of how restructuring can have a direct impact on people's lives at the most local scale (Leach and Winson).

Finally, a significant point implicit in the essays comes from the authors' collective reminder that the impact of restructuring within societies does not fall evenly, either in spatial or societal terms. There is indeed an emerging human geography of difference, for both society and its institutions restructure at different rates and with different consequences in different regions and localities. This conclusion stresses the underlying issue that there is a need to be situated in time and space, with respect for different scales of community and various criteria for community membership, and with a concern for theory and conceptualization. In doing so, social scientists will contribute all the more effectively to the evolving debate on public policy in restructuring societies.

REFERENCES

Agnew, J. (1987), *Place and Politics: The Geographical Mediation of State and Society* (London: Allen and Unwin).

Allen, J., and C. Hamnett, eds. (1995), *A Shrinking World? Global Unevenness and Inequality* (Oxford: Oxford University Press).

Blank, R.H. (1994), *New Zealand Health Policy: A Comparative Study* (Auckland: Auckland University Press).

Brisken, L. (1994), "Equity and Economic Restructuring in the Canadian Labour Movement," *Economic and Industrial Democracy*, vol. 15, no. 1, 89-112.

Britton, S.G., R. Le Heron, and E. Pawson, eds. (1992), *Changing Places in New Zealand: A Geography of Restructuring* (Christchurch: New Zealand Geographical Society).

Chalmers, A.I., and A.E. Joseph (forthcoming), "Rural Change and the Elderly in Rural Places: Commentaries from New Zealand," *Journal of Rural Studies.*

Clark, G.L. (1992), "Real Regulation: The Administrative State," *Environment and Planning A*, vol. 24, no. 5, 615-27.

Creese, G. (1995), "Gender Equity or Masculine Privilege? Union Strategies and Economic Restructuring in a White Collar Union," *Canadian Journal of Sociology*, vol. 20, no. 2, 143-66.

Demko, G.J., and W.B. Wood, eds. (1994), *Reordering the World: Geopolitical Perspectives on the 21st Century* (Boulder, CO: Westview).

Easton, B. (1997), *The Commercialisation of New Zealand* (Auckland: Auckland University Press).

Eisenstadt, S.N. (1966), *Modernization: Protest and Change* (Englewood Cliffs NJ: Prentice-Hall).

Garrick, N., ed. (1998), *Geopolitics and Globalization in a Postmodern World* (Haifa: University of Haifa for the International Geographical Union Commission on the World Political Map).

Geographical Review (1997), vol. 87, no. 2. Special issue on "Cyberspace and Geographical Space."

Giddens, A. (1984), *The Constitution of Society* (Cambridge: Polity Press).

———— (1991), "Structuration Theory: Past, Present and Future," in *Gidden's Theory of Structuration: A Critical Appreciation*, G.A. Bryant and D. Jary, eds. (London: Routledge), 201-21.

Grand Council of the Crees (1998), *Never Without Consent: James Bay Crees' Stand Against Forcible Inclusion into an Independent Québec* (Toronto: ECW Press).

Harvey, D.W. (1989), *The Condition of Postmodernity* (Oxford: Blackwell).

Hoffman, P. (1962), *World Without Want* (London: Chatto and Windus).

James, A.M., and R. Jackson, eds. (1993), *States in a Changing World* (Oxford: Oxford University Press).

Jameson, F. (1991), *Postmodernism* (London: Verso).

Jensen, J. (1995), "Mapping, Naming and Remembering: Globalization at the End of the Twentieth Century," *Review of International Political Economy*, vol. 2, no. 1, 96-116.

Johnston, R.J., P.J. Taylor, and M.J. Watts, eds. (1995), *Geographies of Global Change: Remapping the World in the Late Twentieth Century* (Oxford: Blackwell).

Joseph, A.E., and A.I. Chalmers (1995), "Growing Old in Place: A View from Rural New Zealand," *Health and Place*, vol. 1, no. 2, 79-90.

———— (1996), "Restructuring Long-term Care and the Geography of Ageing: A View from Rural New Zealand," *Social Science and Medicine*, vol. 42, no. 6, 887-96.

Joseph, A.E., and R.A. Kearns (1996), "Deinstitutionalization Meets Restructuring: The Closure of a Psychiatric Hospital in New Zealand," *Health and Place*, vol. 2, no. 3, 179-89.

Joseph, A.E., and D.R. Phillips (1984), *Accessibility and Utilization: Geographical Perspectives on Health Care Delivery* (London: Harper and Row).

Kearns, R.A. (1991), "The Place of Health in the Health of Place: The Case of the Hokianga Special Medical Area," *Social Science and Medicine*, vol. 33, no. 4, 519-30.

————, and J.R. Barnett (1992), "Enter the Supermarket: Entrepreneurial Medical Practice in New Zealand," *Environment and Planning C: Government and Policy*, vol. 10, no. 3, 267-81.

Kearns, R.A., and A.E. Joseph (1997), "Restructuring Health and Rural Communities in New Zealand," *Progress in Human Geography*, vol. 21, no. 1, 18-32.

Kearns, R.A., and J.A. Reinken (1994), "Out for the Count? Questions Concerning the Population of the Hokianga," *New Zealand Population Review*, vol. 20, no. 1, 19-30.

Keith, M., and S. Pile, eds. (1993), *Place and the Politics of Identity* (London: Routledge).

Kelsey, J. (1997), *The New Zealand Experiment: A World Model for Structural Adjustment?*, 2nd edn. (Auckland: Auckland University Press).

Knight, D.B. (1982), "Identity and Territory: Geographical Perspectives on Nationalism and Regionalism," *Annals of the Association of American Geographers*, vol. 71, no. 4, 514-32.

———— (1983), "The Dilemma of Nations in a Rigid State-Structured World," in *Pluralism and Political Geography: People,*

Territory and State, N. Kliot and S. Waterman, eds. (London: Croom Helm), 114-37.

Knight, D.B. (1985), "Territory and People, or People and Territory: Thoughts on Postcolonial Self-Determination," *International Political Science Review*, vol. 6, no. 2, 248-72.

——— (1988), "Self-Determination for Indigenous Peoples: The Context for Change," in *Nationalism, Self-Determination and Political Geography*, R.J. Johnston, D.B. Knight and E. Kofman, eds. (London: Croom Helm), 117–34.

——— (1994), "People Together, Yet Apart: Rethinking Territory, Sovereignty, and Identities," in *Reordering the World: Geopolitical Perspectives on the 21st Century*, G.J. Demko and W.B. Wood, eds. (Boulder CO: Westview), 71-86.

——— (1998a), "Bounding Whose Territory?: Potential Conflict Between a State and a Province Desiring Statehood," in *Geopolitics and Globalization in a Postmodern World*, N. Garrick, ed. (Haifa: University of Haifa for the International Geographical Union Commission on the World Political Map), 57-58.

——— (1998b), "Extending the Local: The Small Town and Globalization," *GeoJournal* [special issue on globalization], vol. 45, nos. 1-2, 145-49.

Le Heron, R., and E. Pawson, *Changing Places: New Zealand in the Nineties* (Auckland: Longman Paul).

Lovering, J. (1989), "The Restructuring Debate," in *New Models in Geography*, vol. 1, R. Peet and N. Thrift, eds. (London: Unwin Hyman), 198-223.

Macdonald, M. (1995), "Economic Restructuring and Gender in Canada: Feminist Policy Initiatives," *World Development*, vol. 23, no. 11, 2005-17.

Malcolm, L., and P. Barnett (1994), "New Zealand's Health Providers in an Emerging Market," *Health Policy*, vol. 29, no. 1, 85-100.

Massey, D. (1991), "The Political Place of Locality Studies," *Environment and Planning A*, vol. 23, no. 2, 267-81.

———, and P. Jess, eds. (1995), *A Place in the World? Places, Cultures and Globalization* (Oxford: Oxford University Press).

O'Hare, N. (1994), "Our Small Towns Fight for their Health," *New Zealand Listener*, 9-15 July, 18-24.

O'Loughlin, J., and H. van der Wusten, eds. (1993), *The New Political Geography of Eastern Europe* (London: Belhaven).

Paasi, A. (1996), *Territories, Boundaries and Consciousness* (Chichester and New York: Wiley, Belhaven Studies in Political Geography).

Pinch, S.P. (1989), "The Restructuring Thesis and the Study of Public Services," *Environment and Planning A*, vol. 21, no. 7, 905-26.

———— (1997), *Worlds of Welfare: Understanding the Changing Geographies of Social Welfare Provision* (London: Routledge).

Pupo, N., and J. White (1994), "Union Leaders and the Economic Crisis: Responses to Restructuring," *Industrial Relations*, vol. 49, no. 4, 821-45.

Rae, B. (1996), *From Protest to Power: Personal Reflections on a Life in Politics* (Toronto: Viking).

Rostow, W. (1960), *The Stages of Economic Development* (Cambridge: Cambridge University Press).

Sayer, R.A. (1985), "Industry and Space: A Sympathetic Review of Radical Research," *Environment and Planning D: Society and Space*, vol. 13, no. 1, 3-29.

Sun Times, Various issues (Owen Sound, Ontario).

Taylor, P.J. (1999), *Modernities: A Geohistorical Interpretation* (Cambridge: Polity Press; Minneapolis: University of Minnesota Press).

————, M.J. Watts, and R.J. Johnston (1995), "Global Change at the End of the Twentieth Century," in *Geographies of Global Change: Remapping the World in the Late Twentieth Century*, R.J. Johnston, P.J. Taylor and M.J. Watts, eds. (Oxford: Blackwell), 1-10.

Thrift, N. (1995), "A Hyperactive World," in *Geographies of Global Change: Remapping the World in the Late Twentieth Century*, R.J. Johnston, P.J. Taylor, and M.J. Watts, eds. (Oxford: Blackwell), 18-35.

Wallace, A.I., and D.B. Knight (1996), "Societies in Space and Place," in *Earthly Goods: Environmental Change and Social Justice*, F.O. Hampson and J. Reppy, eds. (Cornell: Cornell University Press), 75-95.

2

TWO MEN AGAINST REVOLUTION
EDMUND BURKE AND GEORGE ORWELL

Bob Rae

IT MIGHT, AT FIRST BLUSH, seem strange to lump the founder of modern conservatism, Edmund Burke, and one of the great radical voices of the 20th century, George Orwell, in the same pot. There is, indeed, much that divides them. Burke was a politician and a parliamentarian who believed profoundly in the importance of social and political order. An Irishman who was proud of his origins and prouder still of his association with the architects of the Whig Party in Westminster in the middle of the 18th century, Burke was at once a party insider and a philosopher keen to speak to first principles and the broader context of human endeavour.

George Orwell, born Eric Blair, went to Eton and then went to work for the Empire in Burma. Profoundly disillusioned, he returned to England in his late twenties, and decided to become a writer and a witness to the politics of the 20th century. After tramping around England and France, experiences he wrote about in *Down and Out in Paris and London* and *The Road to Wigan Pier*, he fought in Spain on behalf of the Republicans. While in Barcelona, he came to the grim realization that the Communist Party and its supporters worldwide would go to any lengths to achieve monopoly power. They would crush opposition as surely as any capitalist dictatorship. This insight produced *Homage to Catalonia*, which marked Orwell's break with the left-wing orthodoxies of the day.

He was further disillusioned by the signing of the Molotov-Ribbentrop Pact in 1939, and after working for the BBC during the war, wrote two remarkable novels, *Animal Farm* and *1984*. George Orwell died of tuberculosis at the age of 46, still considering himself to be a socialist, certainly a profound democrat, and someone who would probably be surprised to hear himself described in the same breath as Edmund Burke.

Yet there are persistent, fascinating parallels between these two great men. They were both gifted writers, probably the greatest political writers in the English language of their age. Their capacity for irony, invective analysis, and humour have few equals. They both recognized that politics and public life were about great questions. They both had the gift of insight into the challenges of their time. And they were both unafraid to take on the "smelly little orthodoxies" of the day on behalf of the cause of freedom and civility, regardless of party loyalties and the tyranny of conventional opinion.

Above all, they both recognized in the political revolutions that marked their lives something profoundly malicious, which had to be spoken about without fear or favour. They learned that in the making of public policy, narrow ideologies and revolutions of whole cloth were to be despised and rejected. All revolutions, in Burke's phrase, "contain in them something of evil." They produce no lasting good and do much harm. They reject facts and experience in the name of a theory. This is something Burke knew with his very soul. It was something Orwell had to come to, seared by the experience of Spain, World War II, and the overwhelming evidence of human disaster under Stalin and Hitler.

Burke spoke compellingly of the advantages of political parties, and of their importance in the emerging constitution of Great Britain. Burke's defence of party — in *Thoughts on Present Discontents* (1770) — is worth remembering today:

When men are not acquainted with each other's principles, nor experienced in each other's talents, nor at all practised in their mutual habitudes and dispositions by joint efforts of business; no personal confidence, no friendship, no common interest subsisting among them; it is evidently impossible that they can act a public part with uniformity, perseverance, or efficacy.... [T]hat no men could act with effect who did not act in concert; that no men could act in concert, who did not act with confidence; and that no men could act with confidence, who were not bound together by common opinions, common affections, and common interests (Quoted in Morley, 1879, 54).

Had Burke died before 1789, he would be remembered as the boon companion of Fox and Sheridan, the scourge of the Tories, the enemy of Warren Hastings, and the intellectual architect of the modern Whig party. As we all know, this is not what happened. Burke lived to the end of the 1790s, which meant that he had to confront the central political question of his day, the French Revolution.

The conventional view among British liberals was that the French Revolution was an event to be supported, even celebrated. An irrational, corrupt ancient regime was being replaced. Whatever violence and excesses existed were ultimately less important than the objective of an emerging democracy. Certainly this was Charles James Fox's view, and it was widely held among the English progressive intelligentsia.

From the earliest days of the revolution in 1789, Burke took a completely different position. When he was asked for his opinion by a young French nobleman, Burke did so with gusto in his *Reflections on the Revolution in France*. It remains his best known work.

Burke insisted that there was nothing liberal or progressive in what was happening in France. He saw in it something sinister: a mass revolution which could only lead in one direction, to an ideological and military dictatorship.

Burke insisted that those who saw the revolution as part of the liberal tradition were naive at best. This was not the ultimate expression of liberalism; this was its very antithesis, in which liberal ideals of freedom, balance, and civility would all be sacrificed on an ideological altar of a very different nature. Burke's Whig contemporaries were appalled by his reflections. His break with his political friends of thirty years was profound. He died at the end of the decade a solitary figure.

Yet looking back now it is hard not to admire his insight. His view of events seems even more compelling than, say, that of Thomas Paine, who brought out his own broadside *The Rights of Man* in response to Burke. Paine, it is worth recalling, spent months languishing in a French prison as the revolution took its vicious course in 1793 and 1794. While Paine's defence of democracy is eloquent, it is hard not to see something more profound in Burke's comment that:

Of this I am certain, that in a democracy, the majority of the citizens is capable of exercising the most cruel oppressions upon the minority, whenever strong divisions prevail in that kind of polity, as they often must; and that oppression of the minority will extend to far greater numbers, and will be carried on with much greater fury, than can almost ever be apprehended from the dominion of a single sceptre. In such a popular persecution, individual sufferers are in a much more deplorable condition than in any other. Under a cruel prince they have the balmy compassion of mankind to assuage the smart of their wounds; they have the plaudits of the people to animate their generous constancy under their sufferings: *but those who are subjected to wrong under multitudes, are deprived of all external consolation. They seem deserted by mankind; overpowered by a conspiracy of their whole species* (Burke, 1790, 176).

These last few italicized lines (stress not in the original text) surely point the way to the central tragedy of the 20th century, the loss of life and dignity by millions caught in the web of revolutions, whether of Stalinist or Maoist left or Nazi right. It is hard not to see the parallels with Orwell's terrifying description of totalitarian society in *1984*. Winston Smith, the central figure in Orwell's novel, no doubt felt deserted by mankind, overpowered by a conspiracy of the whole species.

Burke understood far better than his contemporaries that freedom and revolution are ultimately incompatible, and that the natural consequence of the narrow ideological mindset is the destruction of a free society itself. He also understood that freedom and order are not incompatible, but are indeed mutually reinforcing. If order becomes oppressive or irrational, the answer is to change, to improve, to reform, but never to destroy or tear down.

Just as Burke was ostracized by his own party for his insights, so, too, in our own century Orwell was pilloried on the left for his "premature" understanding of the despicable tyranny that was Stalinism. He had difficulty getting his books published. "Paper shortages" was even used as an excuse not to print *Animal Farm.*

Luckily Orwell, like Burke before him, was passionately committed to his own insight, and refused to be silenced or bullied. He ultimately did not care for the orthodoxy of conventional opinion, or the personal cost of political isolation.

Here is Orwell on the ultimate similarity between the objectives of Hitler and Stalin:

Simply in the interest of efficiency the Nazis found themselves expropriating, nationalising, destroying the very people they had set out to save. It did not bother them, because their aim was simply power and not any particular form of society. They would just as soon be Reds as the Socialists to the tune of anti-Marxist slogans — well and good, smash the Socialists. If the next step is to smash the capitalists to the tune of Marxist slogans — well and good, smash the capitalists. It is all-in wrestling, and the only rule is to win.

Russia since 1928 shows distinctly similar reversals of policy, always tending to keep the ruling clique in power. As for the hate-campaigns in which totalitarian regimes ceaselessly indulge, they are real enough while they last, but are simply dictated by the needs of the moment. Jews, Poles, Trotskyists, English, French, Czechs, Democrats, Fascists, Marxists — almost anyone can figure as Public Enemy No 1. Hatred can be turned in any direction at a moment's notice, like a plumber's blow-flame (Orwell, *The Collected Essays* ..., vol. 2, 26).

Much ink has been spent these last several years on the question of whether Orwell died a socialist. New evidence has even come to light that he provided intelligence officials with lists of names of Communist Party members and sympathizers. It is hard to understand the surprise or controversy on either point. Orwell was never a Marxist. His loathing of the Communist Party was deep, personal, and predated the McCarthy era by nearly twenty years. He did not say anything, or name anyone privately that he had not done publicly in endless columns and pamphlets.

Orwell's commitment to social democracy was not doctrinal. He hated the English class system, unqualified privilege, and the hypocrisy of Empire. He admired solidarity and the practical values of the ordinary citizen. Orwell's final entries to his manuscript note book are dated 17 April 1949. In it he remarks on hearing English upper-class accents from hospital rooms nearby:

And what voices! A sort of over-fedness, a fatuous self-confidence, a constant bah-bahing of laughter abt [*sic*] nothing, above all a sort of heaviness & richness combined with a fundamental ill-will-people who, one instinctively feels, without even being able to see them, are the enemies of anything intelligent or sensitive or beautiful. No wonder everyone hates us so.

He goes on to express a concern about the "greater and ever increasing softness and luxuriousness of modern life" and makes a further comment on the problems facing the Labour Government:

The greatest of all the disadvantages under which the left-wing movement suffers: that being a newcomer to the political scene, & having to build itself up out of nothing, it had to create a following by telling lies. For a left-wing party in power, its most serious antagonist is always its own past propaganda (Orwell, *The Collected Essays* ..., vol. 4, 515).

I can vouch from my own experience of the wisdom of this last insight from Orwell.

Like Paine before him (and in noted contrast to Burke), Orwell's great gift as a pamphleteer was his simplicity. He understood that the abstraction of "propaganda and demotic speech" was designed to obscure and mislead. Words were twisted against themselves. Language was used to hide what was actually being done. We often describe our current political world as Orwellian because we are swamped by messages from politicians that are "hyped" and "spun." We are having to teach our children not to believe what they read and what they hear.

In Orwell's day, the experts at crafting messages with hidden meaning and buried purpose were the propagandists of the totalitarian and left. He wrote before the image makers of modern mass marketing were allowed to operate at full throttle on television. Watching the shifting public mood in response to classic political negative advertising, it is hard to recall Orwell's words: "Hatred can be turned in any direction at a moment's notice, like a plumber's blow-flame." This is an insight that Burke would have understood and agreed with entirely.

What then of the new "revolutionists," the ideologies of the right? What would Burke and Orwell have made of them? They start from many of the same premises as Lenin or Robespierre. They have a theory. They hate the status quo. Everything that exists is terrible and must be torn down. Something new and bold will take its place. I have even heard the phrase "you can't make an omelette without breaking eggs" coming from a young Tory staffer, unaware no doubt that this was Lenin's justification for the evils of his revolution. People are not eggs.

Burke has more in common with modern social democracy than he does with the libertarian excesses of the Progressive Conservative government in Ontario, which is ruling with an almost religious faith in its own "common sense revolution." He believed above all in the sense of mutual obligation that is the heart of community:

Society is indeed a contract. Subordinate contracts for objects of mere occasional interest may be dissolved at pleasure — but the state ought not to be considered as nothing better than a partnership agreement in a trade of pepper and coffee, callico or tobacco, or some other such low concern, to be taken up for a little temporary interest, and to be dissolved by the fancy of the parties. It is to be looked on with other reverence; because it is a partnership in things subservient only to the gross animal existence of a temporary and perishable nature. It is a partnership in all science; a partnership in all art; a partnership in every virtue, and in all perfection. As the ends of such a partnership cannot be obtained in many generations, it becomes a partnership not only between those who are living, but between those who are living, those who are dead, and those who are to be born (Burke, 1790, 194-95).

We need less revolution and more moderation, less a sense of desperate measures and more a sense of steady building. As Burke put it: "you might have repaired those walls; you might have built on those old foundations ... you began ill because you began by despising everything that belonged to you" (Burke, 1790, 121).

Both Burke and Orwell shared the perspective that the real condition of the people mattered far more than any theory, that the affirmation of freedom was the critical buttress against the abuse of power, and that leadership and courage were always necessary when conventional opinion lost its way. Important lessons for our own time.

What separates Burke and the contemporary neoconservative revolutionaries is a profound difference in temperament, a quite different sense in the role of governments and indeed the art of politics itself. In health, education, welfare and municipal reform, the spirit underlying every proposal is a contempt for whatever arrangements have been put in place, and a missionary sense that intense sacrifice must be made today for the benefit of generations yet unborn. Burke understood that "perhaps the only moral trust with any certainty in our hands is the care of our own time."

No doubt Burke's instinct for balance and prudence put him at odds with Orwell's radical sense that old class structures needed to be brought down. But it also separates him from the libertarian impulse that has captured so many right wing governments. Burke was not a statist by any means. But he understood the importance of a strong civil society, efficient government, and a respect for mutual obligation. Like Orwell, he understood the value of solidarity. So should we all.

REFERENCES

Burke, E. (1790), *Reflections on the Revolution in France* (London: Penguin Classics).

Morley, J., ed. (1879), *Burke* (London: Macmillan, 1879).

Orwell, G. (1933), *Down and Out in Paris and London* (London: Gollancz).

Orwell, G. (1937), *The Road to Wigan Pier* (London: Gollancz).
——— (1938), *Homage to Catalonia* (London: Secker and Warburg).
——— (1945), *Animal Farm* (London: Secker and Warburg).
——— (1949), *Nineteen Eighty-Four* (London: Secker and Warburg).
——— (1968), *The Collected Essays, Journalism and Letters* (London: Secker and Warburg).
Paine, T. (1791), *The Rights of Man* (London: Penguin Classics).

3

DEMOCRACY AND GEOGRAPHY IN THE REREGULATION OF NEW ZEALAND

Warren Moran

IN RECENT YEARS, NEW ZEALAND has occupied more space in the international media than any country of similar size that has not been involved in a revolution or some other catastrophic event. Some might say that such international exposure is itself sufficient to verify the success of what Kelsey (1995) has called "the New Zealand experiment." Such free and largely favourable publicity for a small country is invaluable as it attempts to position itself in changing global circumstances. Normally, New Zealand has to achieve its role in international public relations in more limited ways to more limited audiences through achievements such as the success of the All Black rugby team or by winning the America's Cup in yachting. The extent of the social and economic changes in New Zealand in the 1980s and 1990s and the process of their imposition have been labeled a "revolution" by a recent New Zealand television documentary (Russell, 1996). It has established a new national brand and, undoubtedly, this media production will itself be marketed aggressively internationally.

Such international publicity is an indication of the interest in New Zealand's economic and social changes. Other countries, and Canada is one that stands out, are interested because politicians of all persuasions are searching for solutions to the social and economic circumstances of their own jurisdictions in the late 20th century. New Zealand is an obvious place to look because the changes there occurred so rapidly, were so comprehensive and have largely been completed. They may reveal more than in countries where change has been slower and more piecemeal. The New Zealand experience of the 1980s and 1990s is also valuable to other countries because it demands an interpretation of the process by which it occurred and forces comparisons that may be helpful. The changes are now sufficiently advanced that there has been time for research and reflection. Study of the New

Zealand case will alert other countries to both the unstated assumptions of similar projects and alert the electorate to some of the methods that have been used to achieve change.

There are several features unique to New Zealand (or *Aotearoa* to the Indigenous Maori) that caution the uncritical application of its experience to other jurisdictions. New Zealand is a country small in population (3.6 million) with a unitary system of government and no written constitution. Power is, therefore, very centralized. These features have reinforced the interest in New Zealand as an international laboratory for neo-liberal experimentation. This combination of characteristics has particular significance for the regions of New Zealand. The political power of localities and regions is ceded from the centre. New Zealand is also politically unique in that its founding document of 1840 was a treaty between the leaders of Maori and the Crown — the Treaty of Waitangi (Sharp, 1994a). Somewhat paradoxically, this particular feature surfaced as a significant determinant of New Zealand's future during the reform period, emerging from beneath the social democratic consensus of the postwar period.

In this chapter, I argue that the New Zealand experiment was a project, an orchestrated and systematic effort to change the way in which New Zealand's society and economy is regulated (Moran, *et al.*, 1996). It has sometimes been painted as a deregulation, but I maintain that it is better characterized as a *re*regulation, a change in the manner and nature of regulation. I also argue that in achieving these changes in regulation, groups within society have been affected differently. That the set of changes was a political exercise, with the winners and losers coming from different groups in society, hardly seems surprising. Yet the changes have been painted as something else. The reforms have been legitimized largely by arguments for their economic necessity (Bertram, 1993). They were initiated under a left-wing (Labour) government and later supported and extended by a right-wing (National) government, thus confusing the political motivation for the reforms.

CHARACTERISTICS OF THE REFORM PROJECT

The critical literature expresses little doubt that the reform program represented a neo-liberal political project, and the architects of the program use similar notions of agenda and project, although expressed as a "project of national interest" (see Douglas, 1993). It is possible to identify six characteristics of this process that were particularly important: the dominance of economics within politics and the complementary rise of neo-liberalism; the importance of words and labels in achieving this dominance; the adoption of principles of government involvement and organization that complemented these first two; the incorporation of private-sector advertising and public relations techniques into government; the erosion of democratic ideals in the process of reform; and the importance of individual commitment in defining and driving the project.

Economic arguments were the basis of the reforms, their central tenet being an unbridled faith in the market (Boston, 1991a). By opening New Zealand's capital and commodity markets to international competition and disengaging government from resource control a stronger economy would emerge. Coupled with this economic liberalism was a faith in what Hunt (1996) has labeled "responsibilization of the self." Individuals acting in their own self-interest will achieve optimal resource allocation solutions, and thus, by extension, optimum social arrangements (Treasury, 1984). Governments should interfere as little as possible with the choices of their citizens. The adoption of these neo-liberal tenets was not confined to production. They became the guiding hand for all activities including health and education (Bates, 1990). The strength of commitment to the market as a policy instrument is illustrated by the prohibition of the word "planning" in government circles. In 1996 the distaste was sufficiently strong to change the name of the Planning Tribunal — the body that hears all disputes involving local and regional environmental management and planning-related issues — to the Environment Court.

An important temporal connection was the coincidence of the government reforms with the Uruguay round of GATT. During the 1980s, as a leader of the Cairns group, New Zealand was at the forefront of arguing for eliminating barriers to international trade in agricultural products. The arguments that were developed in this forum were consistent with the doctrine that the country should have a more open economy in all ways. For New Zealand to argue successfully for other countries to eliminate their barriers to agricultural trade, it then needed to show the way by opening its own markets to a range of other products and services. At the same time, New Zealand was re-exporting the ideas of liberalization drawn from international economic institutions such as the International Monetary Fund (IMF), the Organization for Economic Co-operation and Development (OCED) and the World Bank into international economic forums, after having dutifully reformed its own economy as an experiment.

It is difficult to overestimate the importance of words in establishing the dominance of economic ideas in the political discourse of reform. The theoretical and philosophical positions of the project were created and expressed in a particular language (Sharp, 1994b) that was disseminated through Treasury statements, consultants' reports, and the popular media. It became the language of the technocrat and financial expert mixed with management school jargon and metaphor.

Lewis and Moran (1998) argue that the key terms of the project are instrumental and have economic and actuarial association; examples include reform, efficiency, accountability, competitiveness, performance, return and commercial reality. Some words are lifted from their technical contexts, and thus also from assumptions concerning their meaning, and used alongside more obviously suggestive terms like progress, enterprise, achievement, and success. The word efficiency, for example, is an idealized technical moment in neoclassical economics, yet is suggestive of universally optimal solutions. It has become a central legitimatory concept. A common feature is the reduction of all activity to market process. Participants are "producers" (be they teachers or cricketers), the activity itself is a "product," and skills become "assets" and "people investments."

The dominance of this discourse can be analyzed at two levels — the words used and the criteria adopted to organize and judge institutions of all sorts. Organizations and activities became defined in economic terms. Thus hospitals became Crown Health Enterprises, universities and technical institutes became Tertiary Providers, school committees became Boards of Trustees, and the managers of all organizations became Chief Executive Officers. Everything became a sector and an industry: the health sector, the education sector, the rural sector, the adventure tourism industry, and the sex industry. Almost all organizations began to be audited. More importantly, the ideal form of organization, including the departments and ministries of government, were defined using principles from a narrow range of economic theory.

Boston (1991b) describes the transfer of economic philosophy to administrative restructuring as moving from what he calls a sectoral model toward a functional model. Using 1988 Treasury documents, he identifies the principles that guided the reorganization of the bureaucracy (The State Services Commission) and that were meant to provide state agencies with clear and consistent objectives and a high standard of accountability. Agencies were to have functional integrity (that is, have complementary rather than conflicting objectives); the provision of advice and the delivery of services were to be contestable; functions with conflicting or potentially conflicting objectives were to be located in different agencies; bureaucratic or producer capture was to be minimized, as was the duplication of functions; and resources were to be used economically and efficiently (Boston, 1991b). Not only does this list contain incompatible objectives, but it also does not prioritize them and leaves considerable room for judgement according to individual cases. It represents a narrow and economistic view of the nature of organizations when their reality is much more complicated. These principles have had the effect of moving the organization to behave in the manner suggested by the theory and are likely to be deemed successful only while the theory remains credible.

Coupled with this redefinition and ensuing reorganization was the wholesale adoption of the full array of private-sector techniques for communicating and influencing opinion and attitude. Consultants' reports, public relations and advertising techniques replaced government green and white papers. When the first State Owned Enterprises (SOEs) were established, their launches were orchestrated by media events (see Birchfield and Grant, 1993). Several SOEs quickly became major advertisers on prime time television. The organizations that have remained as government departments or ministries, such as the New Zealand Employment Service, have adopted the same techniques to spread their messages.

Lewis and Moran (1998) argue that in practice, core state reform has led to the construction of a minimalist state, but not to a simple assault on all sites of state power. The reduction in the overall size of the state has masked the redistribution of power within and between institutions, particularly to the benefit of central organizations such as Cabinet, Treasury, the Reserve Bank and the State Services Commission. Institutions charged with financial control have become more powerful, and control has shifted away from functional and institutional logics to administrative and financial control.

The dominance of economic ideology in state and business institutions and in the public sphere has altered the meaning and practices of democracy in New Zealand. It has also promoted a collection of specific narratives, which have undermined social democracy. These extend from the assumptions of the universal self-interested individual and the dismissal of the social unit to politicized expressions of the positions Pavlich (1996) identifies in *Government Management*: inherent government ineptitude; the reconfiguration of liberty as consumer choice; the superiority of technocratic expertise over political solutions; and the myth of apolitical resource allocation.

The central strategy of cumulative and rapid change was profoundly undemocratic. Each new reform reduced the state's command over national resources and the potential for opposition, and added to the momentum of the process. Reform was deliberately swift, decisive, radical and relentless, and it was conducted simultaneously on a number of fronts so as to fragment and overwhelm opposition (Douglas, 1993). The critical literature has dubbed this overall strategy "blitzkrieg" (see Kelsey, 1995). The specific subversions of established checks and balances were manifold, and Kelsey (1993) catalogues manipulations of privileged control of information and associated suppression of public criticism. Birchfield and Grant (1993) describe overt strategies of disinformation and disempowerment in the privatization of forestry, while Butterworth and Tarling (1994) expose the secrecy that pervaded the higher education reforms.

The dominance of Treasury in matters of policy and extensions of its privileged access to information and Cabinet decision making disturbed fragile constitutional balances (see Kelsey, 1993). So, too, did the Labour Party's defection from its established ideological stance, which overturned the democratic traditions of ideological competition, committed opposition and electoral choice (Jesson, 1989; Kelsey, 1995). It also removed a traditional focus for specific oppositions and channels of communication between opposition interests, government and the public (Kelsey, 1993). Opposition was further isolated and disempowered in the new legislation itself, especially the State Sector Act (SSA) and the Employment Contracts Act (ECA) (see Kelsey, 1995).

The extent of individual commitment to the success of the project occasionally emerged as differences among the politicians during the formulation of the project. Then Prime Minister David Lange's much quoted "time for a cup of tea" (and a rethinking of policy direction) at the time in late 1987 that Roger Douglas, his Minister of Finance, had virtually secured political support for a flat income tax is an obvious example (see Russell, 1996). But the full extent of this commitment of both politicians and bureaucrats has emerged in the commentaries that have recently appeared. The television program "Revolution" describes the zeal with which Geoffrey Palmer (the Deputy Prime Minister at the time) and Roderick Dean (the Secretary of the State Services Commission) competed at weekly meetings to see that their imple-

mentation tasks were completed. The power of this practical commitment maintained the momentum established by the ideologues
(Russell, 1996).

THE AGENTS IN THE PROCESS

The actual agents that were essential to the project require more attention. In interpreting the circumstances underlying the introduction of
the reforms, Lewis (1995) identifies three groups of agents as especially influential: Treasury, the Business Roundtable (as an agent of
capital), and the political protagonists themselves. In the briefing
papers provided by Treasury for the incoming 1984 government, its
monetarist position was doctrinaire and united. In these documents,
no room was provided for alternative views or representation of the
rich debates surrounding monetarism over the previous decades.
Commentators such as Boston (1991a) recognize two strands in the
Treasury's enthusiasm for monetarism: its intellectual origins in the
work of Milton Friedman and the Chicago School (the paradigm in
which many of the Treasury economists had been trained) and the
pragmatic need to offer solutions to New Zealand's poor economic
performance, including the role of the public sector.

During the ensuing decade, the position of Treasury became more
deeply entrenched. Once its views were accepted by politicians, no
alternative socioeconomic theory could as easily be made as cohesively
appealing or as consistently argued. Easton (1997) refers to a "tight
prior," whereby this closure enveloped a utilitarian, instrumental ratio-
nality that dismisses all alternative thought as pointless because it will
never be acted upon. Successive Ministers of Finance of different political persuasions became increasingly reliant on the advice and constant
stream of documents originating from Treasury. Shortly, I will discuss
the importance of legislation in entrenching these views. Treasury
functionaries were major architects of much of the legislation over
which they had a strong influence. Their position as bureaucratic
agents of neo-liberalism was reinforced by the similarly monetarist-
influenced control agencies — the Reserve Bank and, after 1986, the
State Services Commission.

The New Zealand Business Roundtable (NZBR) is widely cited as
the single most important institutional expression of capital during the
restructuring period (Codd, *et al.*, 1990; Easton, 1997; Roper and
Rudd, 1993). Its influence continues to be derived from its authority
as the voice of corporate New Zealand, its regular publications, the

press statements and newspaper writings of its executive director, and the regular stream of visitors it sponsors. The views of these visitors have generally supported market-driven economies and monetarist theory. The NZBR has almost always supported the economic reforms and some commentators (such as Jesson, 1989; Kelsey, 1993; 1995) stress its particular influence on Roger Douglas, the Minister of Finance, and other political supporters of the reforms.

The political excesses of the National Government in sponsoring heavy government investment in a series of poorly researched "Think Big Projects" in the late 1970s had exposed the limitations of continuing that course. In particular, it provided the political icon of government interference in the economy that became one of the catch phrases of the reform period: "governments shouldn't pick winners." Unfettered markets and freer movement of international capital were painted as the only alternative to such extreme government involvement. This was quickly translated into the questioning of government involvement in all activities, including health and education.

The political agents of the reforms crossed the political spectrum. There is little doubt that Roger Douglas deserves having his name attached to the reforms. By the time that he was in office, his search for alternatives to the somewhat ad hoc economic policies of his own and other parties had converged toward an artificial separation of economics from politics within a monetarist framework. Even before being part of the 1984 government, as opposition critic on the economy, he was in discussion with members of the Treasury and had a representative seconded to his research group (Oliver, 1989). Once in power, his wholesale endorsement of Treasury documents signaled his conversion to a monetarist point of view. From his own and the Labour Party's perspective, the adoption of a neo-liberal economic perspective was a masterly political move. It not only put Douglas in a powerful position but also captured political ground that was more naturally fitted to the traditional philosophy of the main opposition party. These circumstances were later to partly backfire on Douglas and the party (Kelsey, 1995).

Elsewhere, Lewis and I have argued (Lewis and Moran, 1998) that the tightness of this alliance of interests, cemented by shared interests and faith in neo-liberal ideology, defines the New Zealand restructuring process. We suggest that the career path of economist Roderick Deans represents a revealing case study. Deans spent four years at the IMF before becoming Chief Economist at the Reserve Bank in 1979. By

1984, he was deputy governor before becoming head of the State Services Commission in 1986, then chief executive of the corporatized State Owned Enterprise (SOE) Electricorp, followed by chief executive of the newly privatized and leading corporate profit maker, Telecom, in 1992. Throughout this period, he was an influential member of the Business Roundtable and had close ties with corporate leaders and finance ministers (Kelsey, 1995).

LEGISLATIVE CHANGE

The sequence of legislative changes adopted since 1984 are an effective way of describing and analyzing the nature and extent of the restructuring project. In adopting this approach, I take the view that "real regulation" (Marden, 1992; Clark, 1992) is an effective manner of considering social change and providing evidence that can be related to the more abstract stances of the regulation theorists (Aglietta, 1979; Dale, 1991; Tickell and Peck, 1993). Among economists, considerable debate has surrounded the order in which the reforms were undertaken. The politicians' commentaries emphasize the opportunism of many of the changes that they undertook. They looked to leap through windows of opportunity whenever these were opened. What is more remarkable is that the changes occurred over the parliamentary terms of two different parties without the sequence and pace of the reforms being reduced.

Four main phases are recognizable in the sequence of the legislation (Table 1). The tone for the subsequent sequence was set in 1984 at the very beginning of the fourth Labour Government's term. The first phase began when the Government's market liberalization was heralded by an immediate devaluation and floating of the exchange rate partly forced on it by the actions of the previous government and Prime Minister (Easton, 1997). The Government quickly established its seriousness and credibility. Its commitment to trade liberalization was also signalled by removing subsidies for agriculture at an early stage. It increased the pace of tariff reduction and the removal of other regulations protecting New Zealand's manufacturing industries, which had largely grown up in an artificial environment.

The second phase, one of reregulation, distinguished those activities which were not seen as essential responsibilities of government or could be better operated by the private sector. Some state assets, such as forestry production and processing and the Bank of New Zealand,

TABLE I

A PERIODIZATION OF THE NEW ZEALAND REFORMS
1984-95

Restructuring Phase	Electoral Cycle (Government *)	Key Policy Initiatives and Legislation	Activities
Market Liberalization	1984-86 (Labour)	Budget statements, 1984-85 Free float of exchange rate, 1985 Commerce Act, 1986	"Deregulation" of import substitution industries, agriculture and capital markets.
Corporatization / Privatization	1986-88 (Labour)	State Owned Enterprise Act, 1986 plus individual enterprise enabling Acts (Environment, Bank of New Zealand Postal Services)	Restructuring of state trading activities (forestry, banking, telecommunications, utilities).
Core Public Sector Reform	1988-93 (Labour, National)	State Sector Act, 1988 Reserve Bank Act, 1989 Local Government Amendment Act, 1988 Public Finance Act, 1989 Resource Management Act, 1991	Restructuring of central government administrative machinery, health, education, social welfare, and local government.
Entrenchment	1991-96 (National)	Employment Contracts Act, 1991 Fiscal Responsibility Act, 1994 Local Government Law Reform Bill, 1994	Radical reform of industrial relations, and changes to local government. Specific contests over producer boards, Planning Tribunal, superannuation, accident compensation.

* Governing party and term of government
Sources: Kelsey (1995); and Le Heron and Pawson (1996).

were quickly identified as not to be part of the government's role and were prepared for sale. Others were classified as State Owned Enterprises, which under the new Act were to be run as businesses with profit the primary motive. For many of these, this was a preliminary stage before later privatization.

In the third stage, attention focused more intensely on the functioning of government itself. The much publicized Reserve Bank Act set a boundary of two percent inflation as the main performance criterion in the Governor's contract. The State Sector Act, Public Finance Act and later the Fiscal Responsibility Act used legislation to attempt to bring similar fiscal, contractual and other constraints to the departments and ministries of government as those that were presumed to exist in the private sector. Toward the end of the third phase (in 1990), the Labour Government was defeated, in part due to internal disagreement over proceeding to the fourth stage of the process: entrenching the reforms to date through labour market reform and significant public expenditure cuts. When the reformists lost control of the Labour Government, corporate capital abandoned the Party and returned their support to the National Party, the natural party of the right. Labour market reform was the ultimate goal for capital (just as it was for farmers), and they looked to the National Party to reinvigorate the reform process and deliver it. The Employment Contracts Act sits uneasily across the boundaries of the third and fourth phases, and underlines the importance of the change in government in 1990.

The ideological purity of the process was intensified under the National Government. In particular, it introduced the Employment Contracts Act which emphasized individual enterprise-based contracts for workers and weakened the power of the unions. It is unlikely that such legislation would have been successful under a Labour government. The full set of principles that had driven the reforms of central government were applied progressively to local government in the last two phases.

SITES OF RESISTANCE

The reforms have not been without resistance, although, given their reach, much less than might be expected. Two sites of resistance are discussed here as illustrations of the texture and contradictions of the reforms — the continuing resistance offered by the Producer Marketing Boards and the particular role played by Maori during the reforms.

Since the 1930s, New Zealand agricultural products have been marketed internationally by statutory boards. These boards have the legislative right to become fully involved in the acquisition and distribution of their commodities, although only the New Zealand Dairy Board, Apple and Pear Marketing Board and Kiwifruit Marketing Board have exercised this fully (Moran, *et al.*, 1996). In conception they are similar to the Canadian Wheat Board. From the beginning of the reforms, the monopolistic power of the producer boards came under scrutiny and attack. The briefing document presented by Treasury to the 1984 incoming Labour Government severely questioned the power of the boards, and orchestrated critiques continued from a variety of sources during the 1980s and 1990s. Despite these expressions of disapproval, the Kiwifruit Marketing Board was established in 1988 by government at the request of growers.

Four groups have been vociferous in their criticism of the producer marketing boards — the Treasury, some members of the government caucus, the New Zealand Business Roundtable and corporate agriculturalists. Treasury has consistently argued for the removal of the legislation supporting producer marketing boards claiming that it distorts markets and gives the wrong signals to producers. Despite support for this position from Members of Parliament across the political spectrum, few changes in the power of marketing boards have occurred (the relaxation of the internal marketing of apples is one exception). In the case of the more general power of the boards, the ideological statements of Treasury, supported by very little hard evidence, have been insufficient to offset the political support of farmers for them. The National government has not been confident enough in its position to risk loss of the farm vote.

The most aggressive campaigners against the producer marketing boards have been the NZBR and a corporate apple and dairy farmer, Applefields. With the institutional and research support of the NZBR, Applefields ran a long campaign in the early 1990s to break the monopoly of the Apple and Pear Marketing Board. It used the new Commerce Act to bring cases against the Board while applying for licences to export apples on its own behalf. After a series of attempts, it was unsuccessful. The government of the time went as far as amending the legislation to ensure that the producer marketing boards were not fully subject to the Commerce Act. The NZBR has orchestrated similar assaults against the other boards. It commissioned an extensive treatise on the evils of the boards, and their inappropriateness in a neoclassical economic order. In an outburst typical of the Roundtable's regular media forays into the producer board debate and, indeed, any issues of current social and economic significance, executive director Roger Kerr responded to the publication of research commissioned by the Apple and Pear Marketing Board which, understandably, supported the concept of marketing boards. He wrote in a weekly newspaper:

Cost padding and lack of innovation are problems typically associated with restrictions on competition. Granted a quiet life, producer boards could be expected to engage in wasteful capital expenditure, pay excessive salaries relative to the performance of staff, fail to take entrepreneurial risks, stay at the commodity end of the business rather than concentrate on value-added and consumer products, and the like.... The basic point is that seeking views in these industries through political processes — referenda and the like — makes no sense as a way of deciding the commercial rules that should apply to them. The only point of principle that should concern policy makers is whether there is any reason to deny individuals or firms whose business doesn't interfere with anyone else's the normal commercial freedom to sell what they produce to buyers of their choice, including overseas buyers. In any free enterprise system, numbers shouldn't even enter the picture. (*The Independent*, February 23, 1996, 110)

The NZBR was also involved in supporting a move by Maori growers to exempt themselves from the Kiwifruit Marketing Board's single seller monopoly under the Treaty of Waitangi Act. This would have made the future of the monopoly untenable. It was a fascinating use of legislation in part designed to secure for Maori the resources to resist the onslaught of corporate capitalism. Two one-time Ministers of Finance, Ruth Richardson and the newly knighted Sir Roger Douglas, appeared as expert witnesses for the plaintiffs, and an ex-Prime Minister, Sir Geoffrey Palmer, as Council. This latest rearrangement of the personalities, ideology, processes and opportunism that have characterized the reforms, illuminates again the nature of the project.

The attempt to co-opt sites of resistance, such as among Maori, is particularly revealing. It was significant in the education and health reforms, where existing dissatisfactions were used to justify a single option for change, and more obvious in the reregulation of land use and the distraction of the environmental movement by the Resource Management Act (RMA) (Memon and Gleeson, 1995). Senior executive contracts in the public sector "bought" compliance with high salaries, while individual contracts and new formal accountability and employment structures have replaced civil service loyalties throughout the state. Efforts to seal Maori claims against the Crown beneath a predetermined cap have also been made with the aim of turning future Maori resistance inward.

Early in its term, in 1984, the Labour Government amended the Treaty of Waitangi legislation to permit Maori to bring claims, for land

and other grievances from as far back as 1840, before the Waitangi Tribunal. It is plausible that this amendment and its results will in the long term be seen as the main contribution of that government to New Zealand society, rather than its economic reforms. Indeed, Maori have been successfully bringing substantial claims parallel with the reforms. Some of the more notable of these include the Tainui settlement in 1995 worth a purported NZ$170 million, and the Sealord Fisheries deal that settled Maori fisheries claims and transferred an estimated NZ$400 million in quota and assets from the Maori Fisheries Commission to Te Ohu Kai Moana in 1992 (see Kelsey, 1995, 320). This settlement established a model for the fiscal envelope arrangements. The Tribunal has recently given its support to a NZ$140 million claim by one Maori group, Muriwhenua, for the Te Aupouri forests and other land assets of up to 170,000 hectares in Northland, and has threatened to use its powers to force the return of state forest to Maori ownership for the first time.

The aspirations of Maori and the claims facilitated by the 1985 legislation have had a direct relationship to the economic reforms. Maori led the most effective legal challenges to the government decision to privatize the state's one million hectares of plantation forests. They argued that some of the lands on which the forests were planted were likely to have been wrongly appropriated. If such land were sold, the Maori case against the Crown would be compromised by private ownership. On these grounds, the Maori Council successfully brought a case to the High Court against the sale of forestry land. This forced the government to compromise by agreeing to sell the cutting rights to the trees rather than the land itself and to include provisions for a reconsideration of the profits from the sale if subsequent treaty claims were successful. As part of the negotiations, a fund was established for research on behalf of Maori on the transactions that led to the Crown ownership of the forest land.

Maori have been close to the reforms in other ways too. Their lower than average socioeconomic status and concentration in regions and occupations adversely affected by job loss and squeezed wages and working conditions have seen them bear a disproportionate share of the losses under the reforms. In some industries such as forestry, where Maori had made their careers in the state service, many joined the unemployment queues. More recent reform initiatives, such as benefit cuts and raising state housing rents to market rates, have also affected Maori severely. The result has been a reverse migration of Maori away from the urban areas to their rural ancestral lands (see Blunden, *et al.*, 1996).

Paradoxically, at the same time, the corporatization and privatization programs coupled with the Treaty of Waitangi Amendment Act (1985) have forced a confrontation with Maori claims, thereby releasing land and financial resources to Maori. The restructuring of virtually all of the state services exposed further tracts of Crown-held land to these processes. Much of this former state land was sold on the open market, but in areas where claims were successful, a proportion of it has been used to settle treaty claims. This would not have been possible without the state divesting itself of many of its assets, including land. A notional sum of one billion dollars was made available by the National Government within a "fiscal envelope" to settle all Maori claims against the Crown. This cap is now seen as a "bottom line" as tribes manoeuver to settle claims.

It is difficult to imagine this redistribution of funds to Maori without the reforms as not only have they helped fund the settlements, but they have also resulted in the formal valuation of state assets and established a culture of multi-million dollar state deals. Yet, while this Maori resistance has been effective in securing gains for Maori, it has failed to slow the reforms generally or, indeed, restrict later asset sales (such as cutting rights to the vast Kaingaroa forests, which were sold in late 1996).

GEOGRAPHY OF THE REFORMS

Elsewhere, I have argued that a reshaped geography has been an integral part of the reforms (Moran, 1995). Not only has the social and economic geography of the nation been changed by the reforms, but space was used to effect the reforms (Lefebvre, 1991). In the reorganization of many departments and ministries of government, a central issue became the extent to which the organizations of central government would be represented in the regions. Given that each agency was acting on its own behalf, a plethora of new regional structures was created. Some of the other results are thoroughly documented in the volume *Changing Places* (Le Heron and Pawson, 1996).

The geographies of the reregulated activities necessitated different structures. These had to be reconciled with managerial principles that the government had set for the reorganization of the core state, such as the separation of policy from its implementation and a parallel separation of the purchasing of a service from its delivery. Thus, in terms of health care, four Regional Health Authorities (RHAs) were created in 1993 whose function was to purchase health services from clusters of public hospitals relabeled as Crown Health Enterprises (CHEs), within a framework of competitive bidding for service contracts (Kearns and Joseph, 1997). The role of the Ministry of Health was confined to one of a source of policy advice to the Minister. From time to time, the number of RHAs has become an issue. In a sense, the RHAs were a means of distancing the government from difficult decisions about health. But if they were reduced to as few as two, which was suggested, the more direct relation of the RHAs to government would become apparent. Any reduction was resisted until pressure on the National-led coalition government formed after the first Mixed-Member Proportional representation (MMP) election in 1996 led to the establishment of a Transitional Health Authority (THA). The THA is charged with overseeing the move back to a co-ordinated, national approach to the funding and purchase of services in the public health sector.

In education, the relationship between central authority and locality have become much more direct. Parents with children attending a school were eligible to be elected to small Boards of Trustees, which became responsible for school policy. Part of the objective of government was to fund these Boards directly, including for teachers' salaries. This "bulk funding" of schools remains widely opposed by the teachers' unions, which continue to see it as a direct threat to their nationally negotiated salaries, and as a clear opportunity for government to squeeze education funding and, ultimately, impose a market system in a similar inexorable process to that directed at universities. In the reorganization of the education sector, and in contrast to health care, any regional representation of the Ministry of Education largely disappeared. As with health, the matter of who was really in control became an issue. Authority without finance in a system that has always been funded from central government hardly meant more local autonomy. Schools, however, are encouraged to pursue their own sources of finance via fees and full fee-paying foreign students in particular. Indeed, many secondary schools are now reliant on this "export" of education (Dale and Robertson, 1996). This central control has been tightened under the reforms by the creation of a new monitoring agency (the Education Review Office), whose primary function is to ensure compliance with the new managerial regulations rather than inspect the quality of the education experience. A New Zealand

Qualifications Authority (distinct from the Ministry of Education) has also been created, which has instituted a series of Unit Standards for all subjects and qualifications. These represent another new, invasive and relatively rigid regulatory form, controlled from the centre, which has gone beyond its original intention to replace examinations. Other new regulations and measures, including the contract between parents and government established by the Education Charter, and the introduction of sets of national guidelines overriding local policy, and a new curriculum framework, also go beyond the original stated intent of the reforms.

The abolition of school zoning has seen a pseudo-market develop where schools compete for students (hopefully higher calibre and richer students) and funding, which is tied to student numbers. For fortunate schools, this may then induce a positive feedback spiral of rising standards and a demand for places articulated by parents. Yet, it is not surprising that the earliest indications of this demand operating in practice are the reverse processes of spirals of decline. Neither is it surprising that these are occurring in areas of socioeconomic deprivation with high concentrations of Maori and Pacific Islanders. Additional state funding is provided by a formula dependent on the socioeconomic status of the locality, a circumstance not unfamiliar in Canada. Authorities claim that this offers some protection against the spiral of decline for schools with lesser reputations and poor national examination results.

The theme that connects these patterns and ties them to the wider processes of neo-liberal reform is a localization of responsibility (and the legitimatory burden) and a centralization of control. Not only is this a set of processes occurring across space and resulting in new sets of spatial patterns, but it deeply involves space in the strategies of reform. Space is used strategically to distance government from legitimation problems, while the shrinking state has transmitted risk and responsibility to the individual and necessitated new regimes of self-governance. Immediate requirements to promote and ensure the self threaten to overwhelm any individual commitment to social democracy. New community-based decision making bodies such as School Boards of Trustees have responsibility but heavily circumscribed powers, separating them from the idealized communities of liberal-humanist discourse.

The reorganization of government departments and ministries also resulted in new regional structures for them. During the 1980s, virtually every government agency was restructured, its procedures, activities and institutional forms altered. This included divesting themselves of certain activities and organizing the department in a manner that complied with the principles discussed earlier (Treasury, 1987a; 1987b). Reorganization reflected an acceptance both of the belief in the inherent spatiality of efficiency (which dictates against the duplication of services) and of the separation of policy from delivery; it also represented new strategic uses of space and responses to the difficult problem of providing services to dispersed populations. In every case this meant a changed relationship with the regions and localities of New Zealand. As might be expected, the dominant result was the closure of regional offices and the loss of close-grained relationships with parts of the country. The only exception was the Department of Conservation which retained a strong regional structure. As this Department was responsible for much land owned by the Crown in different parts of New Zealand, this exception was almost inevitable.

MMP brought its own regional reorganization. The number of constituency seats was reduced to 65 from 99, with a further 60 representatives in the house being selected from party lists. The average size and diversity of electorates has, therefore, increased and the relationship of the regions to the centre has changed. This loss of regional representation is more important in a unitary system of government when much more power is held at the centre. Any devolution of responsibility is at the goodwill of the centre. The style of the central government reforms were also transferred to local authorities which, notwithstanding a long period of often effective resistance, have been transformed in a similar way to central government. In the first instance, they were amalgamated and consolidated, and 22 regions became 12, and 231 local authorities became 60 districts and 12 cities. Activities which are deemed to be best carried out by commercial organizations have been distinguished and either contracted to the private sector (e.g., waste management) or formed into Local Area Trading Organizations, the local equivalent to State Owned Enterprises.

A single region example such as Northland illustrates the effects of the reforms on a region's administrative and economic geography. Local government restructuring reduced the number of local authorities to four district councils — the Far North, Whangarei, Kaipara, and Rodney. Under MMP, the people of Northland will have three direct representatives — one for a seat called Northland, one for Whangarei (the main urban area) and one for a seat called Rodney which symbolically and in terms of regional government is really part of the City of Auckland.

Contemporaneously, the actions of central government restructuring and global industrial reorganization have changed the face of capitalism in New Zealand. The new spatiality arising from increased mobility of capital and new logics of capitalist accumulation (which Castells [1991] argues describe a new space of flows, superseding the space of places) has reorganized activity in the region. A decade ago, the forestry industry of the region was dominated by the state and the New Zealand Forest Products (NZFP) Company. Maori trusts, some joint ventures (NZFP/Shell) and individuals owned the remaining forests. By 1995, ownership of the forests was dominated by American companies. International Paper, through its majority holding of Carter Holt Harvey (which itself acquired NZFP in the fallout of the 1987 share market crash), and ITT Rayonier (through its purchase of the residual state forests), together own about 70 percent of Northland forest. The remainder is owned by Maori, individuals, or small groups. Thus, New Zealand's neo-liberal ideology of the 1980s has facilitated the global aspirations of American companies wishing either to secure supplies of wood internationally (International Paper) or to diversify sectorally and spatially (Rayonier).

ASSESSMENT AND CONCLUSION

Any assessment of the New Zealand experiment depends on the criteria one uses. Almost inevitably, economic criteria become primary. The unstated argument is that economics was the foundation of the reforms and the reforms should therefore be measured against economic criteria.

According to most macroeconomic criteria, the reforms would be judged as successful. National debt has been reduced substantially. Income from the sale of assets has been used mainly to pay off government debt, which has stopped growing now that government is able to balance its budget. Indeed, surpluses are now being achieved and taxes have been cut, and until the National-led coalition government changed priorities, more were planned. These have now been delayed as the coalition partner (the New Zealand First Party) demands more social spending on health and education. Until recently, too, the new underlying inflation measure has been restricted to under the two percent per annum set in the contract of the Governor of the Reserve

Bank. And in the years when it emerged from the recession (1993-95), New Zealand achieved strong rates of growth and unemployment fell rapidly. The former government trading activities, whether they are State Owned Enterprises (such as New Zealand Post) or have been privatized (such as Telecom), are no longer the drain on the public purse that they were in the past. Indeed, they are now contributing to government income, either through their profits as State Owned Enterprises or through the tax system when privatized.

On the other hand, the success is qualified, even by macroeconomic measures alone. The people of New Zealand no longer own the assets concerned, and they cannot be sold again. The rates of economic growth, no more than adequate by the standards of the region, were predicated on extremely low base levels of activity and are forecast to be only between two percent and four percent in the next period. Much of the personal loss of the reform period registered as a deep recession marked by very high unemployment. Higher costs of social welfare and other benefits resulted. Real wages have fallen for many workers, while benefits and social spending have been cut. Total national debt now runs at an all-time high, although it is held predominantly by the private sector. Real interest rates are high and the exchange rate is inflated by these and the speculative advantages afforded by the government's commitment to defend the two percent inflation target.

These new macroeconomic patterns are hurting exporters, particularly those dependent on international commodity price fluctuations. Their difficulties are new expressions of the social cost and personal loss that characterized the reforms, yet were sanitized and disguised by macroeconomic aggregates. Corporatization and privatization, for example, resulted in large numbers of redundancies and considerable personal costs for individuals who had been encouraged to make their careers in the government service and suddenly had no job.

Nevertheless, among the international monetary and economic agencies, New Zealand is something of the teacher's pet. It has instituted the types of reforms that they suggest and their reports give us the credit. Their praise is fulsome. In a paper given early in 1997 in New Zealand, the Deputy Director of the IMF suggested that the approach to controlling reflation in the New Zealand Reserve Bank Act had strong theoretical and practical support. He reported that an increasing number of countries are adopting a similar policy and predicts that many more will join. With that sort of support inside the IMF, his prediction is likely to be proved right.

In the core social services of health and education, the results have been even less clear. Crown Health Enterprises continue to run large deficits and many of them regularly have to make urgent adjustments to their decisions about which patients to treat as they find themselves in financial difficulty. Long waiting lists for elective surgery persist in the public health clinics and hospitals. In education, teacher shortages and crowded schools through the building program being poorly planned and executed have been common. Teachers and parents have expressed their concerns about many aspects of the new system. Some of these relate to the reorganization of the bureaucracy, and the delay, lack of success and professional, philosophical acrimony over the compilation and publication of the new Unit Standards has eroded confidence. Major concerns remain over the development of a two-tier health system (a private system funded by personal insurance and a sub-standard public service) and over similar possibilities in education.

Yet even in health and education there have been some gains. In health, for instance, the new emphasis on measurement, contracts, real costs and pricing, has revealed much more about the economics of health care. The existence of four funding agencies, each negotiating with the local Crown Health Enterprises and private suppliers over the cost of services that are being provided in a range of different contexts, has added to this knowledge. Given that the demands on public health care will continue to escalate, this increase in the understanding of the nature of the health system and its costs will be valuable.

It is inevitable that the strengths and weaknesses of the reforms directly reflect the principles that guided them. When the activity being restructured fits the limited economic and organizational theory that is the basis of the reforms, the results have been relatively successful. When more complex activities, such as those providing social goods, are concerned, any judgement must be more equivocal. If those involved in the provision of health care and education were asked to judge the quality of the present system compared with before the reforms, I suspect that the results would be negative. Certainly, in the regular polls taken to identify the public's main concerns, health and education continue to be top priorities.

My concerns in this paper regarding the intersections of geography, democracy and reregulation inform the new uncertainties that underlie public unease with reforms. The spatiality of the new principles of administrative organization has been elevated to a central role in debates over their democratic implications. Strategies of selective localization and tightened bureaucratic control from the centre have been incorporated into new state forms to encourage the public to reassign risk and responsibility to themselves, while leaving control at the centre. The cancellation of the former social-democratic spatial contract has reformed what were previously geographically defined solutions to questions of access to health care and education. Similarly, the removal of policy functions from the local context, as well as layers of representation and political participation, have contributed to redefinitions of the power to influence personal futures. This is now located more fully and more transparently in the market. It is presented in a rhetoric of aspatiality, and expressed within the central metaphor of the "level playing field." The bumps, slopes and hollows are good grounds for public unease.

REFERENCES

Aglietta, M. (1979), *A Theory of Capitalist Regulation: The U.S. Experience* (London: New Left Books).

Bates, R. (1990), "Educational Policy and the New Cult of Efficiency," in Middleton, *et al.*, eds., *New Zealand Educational Policy Today* (Wellington: Allen and Unwin), 40-52.

Bertram, G. (1993), "Keynesianism, Neo-classicism, and the State," in *State and Economy in New Zealand*, B. Roper and C. Rudd, eds. (Auckland: Oxford University Press), 26-49.

Birchfield, R., and I. Grant (1993), *Out of the Woods: The Restructuring and Sale of New Zealand's State Forests* (Wellington: GP Publications).

Blunden, G., C. Cocklin, W. Smith, and W. Moran (1996), "Sustainability: A View from the Paddock," *New Zealand Geographer*, vol. 52, no. 2, 24-34.

Boston, J., J. Martin, J. Pallot, and P. Walsh, eds. (1991), *Reshaping the State: New Zealand's Bureaucratic Revolution* (Auckland: Oxford University Press).

Boston, J. (1991a), "The Theoretical Underpinnings of Public Sector Restructuring in New Zealand," in *Reshaping the State: New Zealand's Bureaucratic Revolution*, J. Boston, *et al.*, eds. (Auckland: Oxford University Press), 1-26.

——— (1991b), "Reorganizing the Machinery of Government: Objectives and Outcomes," in *Reshaping the State: New Zealand's*

Bureaucratic Revolution, J. Boston, *et al.*, eds. (Auckland: Oxford University Press), 233-67.

Butterworth, R., and N. Tarling (1994), *A Shakeup Anyway: Government and the Universities in New Zealand in a Decade of Reform* (Auckland: Auckland University Press).

Castells, M. (1991), *The Informational City: Information, Technology, Economic Restructuring, and the Urban-Regional Process* (Oxford: Blackwell).

Clark, G. (1992), "'Real' Regulation: The Administrative State," *Environment and Planning A*, vol. 24, no. 5, 615-27.

Codd, J., R. Harker, and R. Nash, eds. (1990), *Political Issues in New Zealand Education*, 2nd edn. (Palmerston North: Dunmore Press).

Dale, R. (1991), "Regulation Theory, Settlements and Education Policy," in *Education Policy and the Changing Role of the State: The Proceedings of the New Zealand Association for Research in Education Seminar on Educational Policy, Massey 1990*, L. Gordon and J. Codd, eds. (Palmerston North: Delta, Massey University), 33-43.

————, and S. Robertson (1996), "Resiting the Nation, Reshaping the State," paper presented at the New Zealand Political Studies Association Conference, Auckland, July 8-10, 1996.

Douglas, R. (1993), *Unfinished Business* (Auckland: Random House).

Easton, B. (1997), *The Commercialisation of New Zealand* (Auckland: Auckland University Press).

Gordon, L., and J. Codd, eds. (1991), *Education Policy and the Changing Role of the State: The Proceedings of the New Zealand Association for Research in Education Seminar on Educational Policy, Massey 1990* (Palmerston North: Delta, Massey University).

Hunt, A. (unpublished), "Governing, Liberalism and the Law," paper presented as part of Foundation Visitor Lecture Series, University of Auckland, July 7-9, 1996.

Jesson, B. (1989), *Fragments of Labour: The Story Behind the Fourth Labour Government* (Auckland: Penguin).

Kelsey, J. (1993), *Rolling Back the State: The Privatization of Power in Aotearoa/New Zealand* (Wellington: Bridget Williams Books).

———— (1995), *The New Zealand Experiment: A World Model for Structural Adjustment* (Wellington: Williams Books).

Lefebvre, H. (1991a), *The Production of Space* (Oxford: Basil Blackwell).

Le Heron, R., and E. Pawson (1996), *Changing Places: New Zealand in the Nineties* (Auckland: Longman Paul).

Lewis, N. (1995), "Geography and the Origins of the Restructuring Metanarrative," paper presented at the New Zealand Geographical Society Conference, Christchurch, August 27-30, 1995.

———, and W. Moran (1998), "Restructuring, Democracy and Geography in New Zealand," *Environment and Planning C: Government and Policy,* vol. 16, no. 2, 127-53.

Marden, P. (1992), "'Real' Regulation Reconsidered," *Environment and Planning A*, vol. 24, no. 5, 751-67.

Memon, A., and B. Gleeson (1995), "Towards a New Planning Paradigm? Reflections on New Zealand's Resource Management Act," *Environment and Planning B: Planning and Design*, vol. 22, no. 1, 109-24.

Moran W. (1995), "Democracy, Geography and Restructuring in New Zealand," paper presented at the New Zealand Geographical Society Conference, Christchurch, August 27-30, 1995.

———, G. Blunden, M. Workman, and A. Bradly (1996), "Family Farmers, Real Regulation and the Experience of Food Regimes," *Journal of Rural Studies*, vol. 12, no. 3, 245-58.

Oliver, W.H. (1989), "The Labour Caucus and Economic Policy Formation, 1981-1984," in *The Making of Rogernomincs*, B. Easton, ed. (Auckland: Auckland University Press), 11-52.

Pavlich, G. (1996), "Governance and Crime Prevention: 'Social' Versus 'Community' Regulation," paper presented to the Law and Society Association Annual Conference, University of Strathclyde, Glasgow, July 10-13, 1996.

Roper, B., and C. Rudd, eds. (1993), *State and Economy in New Zealand* (Auckland: Oxford University Press).

Russell, M. (1996), *Revolution: New Zealand, From Fortress to Free Market* (Auckland: Hodder Moa Beckett).

Sharp, A., ed. (1994a), *Leap Into the Dark: The Changing Role of the State in New Zealand since 1984* (Auckland: Auckland University Press).

——— (1994b), "Pride, Resentment and Change in the State and the Economy," in *Leap Into the Dark: The Changing Role of the State in New Zealand since 1984*, A. Sharp, ed. (Auckland: Auckland University Press), 225-49.

Tickell, A., and J. Peck (1995), "Social Regulation after Fordism:

Regulation Theory, Neo-liberalism and the Global-Local Nexus," *Economy and Society*, vol. 24, no. 3, 357-86.

Treasury (1984), *Economic Management* (Wellington: Government Printer).

——— (1987a), *Government Management*, vol. 1 (Wellington: Government Printer).

——— (1987b), *Government Management*, vol. 2 (Wellington: Government Printer).

4

CHANGING EMPLOYMENT RELATIONS: EMPIRICAL DATA, SOCIAL PERSPECTIVES AND POLICY OPTIONS

Julian Barling

"For the times, they are a-changing" — Bob Dylan

WHEN BOB DYLAN FIRST SANG THESE WORDS in 1964, he was certainly correct. Today, however, with the unprecedented depth and breadth of changes in the workplace coinciding with a change in millennium, his words could not be more prescient. The aim of this chapter is to provide a basis for understanding the nature and meaning of these changes, primarily from the perspective of workers who inhabit our workplaces, and to start to understand how governments, employers, unions, and academics might begin to respond to these changes. To do so, three interrelated issues will be addressed. First, empirical data showing changes in the amount, timing and nature of work are examined. These data are then used to understand how the subjective experience, or quality, of employment has changed. Thereafter, the implications of these changes for policy makers, employers, unions, and academics are considered.

While it is well beyond the scope of this chapter to examine the causes of these changes, we would be remiss if we did not mention some of the primary causal factors. These include substantial growth in technological sophistication and increasing accessibility to the technology, the notion of "just-in-time" production, the practice of "re-engineering," entrenching globalization, and, of course, shrinking budgets and increasing competitiveness. Importantly, these issues do not act in isolation, but instead are interrelated. Thus, as pressure for "just-in-time" manufacturing increases, so does the need for increased technological sophistication. As we move more toward global markets, increased competitiveness gains in importance, and vice versa. Importantly, these complex interactions hasten the rate of change in the amount of work available, and the experience of work.

Just how widespread are these changes? A decade ago, Tom Peters (1988) speculated on the meaning of these changes, and showed how all aspects of work, production and organization had been affected. Over and above changes in manufacturing, he showed how dramatic changes were occurring in marketing functions (increased use of niche markets and advertising), sales and service (e.g., teams), international activity (global manufacturing), innovation (speed), people management (increased use of teams; contingent workers), organizational changes (flatter hierarchies), information technology (decentralized data processing), financial management and control (spending authority delegated to appropriate unit level) and leadership (value driven, visionary leadership). Two points are worth noting. First, these functions are interrelated, and their complex interactions have led to major changes in the amount, timing and distribution of work; it is to an examination of these factors that we now turn our attention. Second, most of these changes are now commonplace.

CHANGES IN THE AMOUNT AND TIMING OF WORK

To understand the enormity of these changes, we will explore shifts in the amount of work, part-time work, self-employment, and unemployment. This will provide the basis for understanding the current subjective experience of work.

The Amount of Full-Time Work

For most of the 20th century, the story about the amount of work employees had to engage in has been very positive, as is evident in the case of workers in manufacturing. In 1901, the average number of hours worked per week was 59, and by 1957 it had dropped dramatically to 40. These changes seemed to occur in spurts (primarily between 1911-21, and again between 1941-51), with most of this decline in place before 1949 (Sunter and Morisette, 1994). After 1960, the downward trend levelled off, so that by the beginning of the 1980s, the average length of the work week for the manufacturing sector had stabilized at around 38 hours.

At about that time, however, the story changes and becomes more complex and diverse. In her book *The Overworked American*, Schorr (1993) showed that there was an increase from 1967 to 1987 both in the average number of hours worked per week (from 39.8 to 40.7), as well as in the number of weeks worked per year (from 43.9 to 47.1). This increase was certainly more pronounced for women for whom the number of hours went from 35.2 to 47, and the number of weeks worked per year from 39.3 to 45.4 (compared with 43.0 to 43.8, and 47.1 to 48.5 respectively, for men). Of course, some of the increase in the amount of work engaged in by women is attributable to the increase of employed mothers in the labour force (see Barling, 1990). More recently, workers report having to work much harder than they had previously (Angus Reid, 1996; Canadian Auto Workers, 1996; Hancock, *et al.*, 1995). Of greater concern from our perspective here, however, is the extent to which employees engage in more (or less) work by choice or not, and we will return to this issue after considering trends in part-time employment.

When considering the amount of time spent working, an additional consideration would be the amount of time devoted on a daily basis to commuting. In 1992, about 25 percent of Canadians spent more than an hour per day commuting to and from work (Marshall, 1994). For residents of Toronto and Vancouver, the average is more than one hour per day; for those in Montreal, Ottawa-Hull and Winnipeg, the daily commute approached one hour. Commuting time is significant inasmuch as commuters increase the amount of time devoted directly or indirectly to work, thereby decreasing the amount of time they have available for non-work pursuits.

One final issue concerns the distribution of the actual number of hours worked over time. Specifically, while the *average* number of hours worked over the past 20 years has remained constant, compositional change has occurred (Cohen, 1991), that is, there has been some change at both extremes of the distribution. As can be seen from Figure 1, more people are now working longer hours, and more people are working fewer hours (Sheridan, Sunter and Diverty, 1996). The extent to which we are now witnessing polarization within the workforce will be examined in more detail later in this chapter.

Part-Time Work

Despite reassurances by politicians about the growth of high-paying, high-quality full-time jobs, the most significant changes to the amount and timing of work relates to non-standard work in general, and part-time work in particular (Krahn, 1995). In fact, part-time jobs more than doubled in Canada between 1975 and 1993, while the rate of

FIGURE I

COMPOSITIONAL CHANGES IN THE NUMBER OF HOURS
WORKED PER WEEK IN CANADA BETWEEN
1976 AND 1996

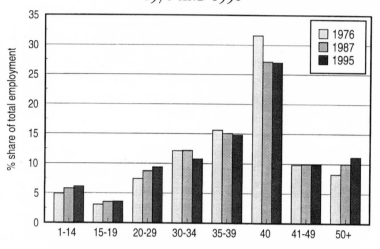

growth of full-time jobs was relatively flat (see Figure 2). While it is obvious that some of the growth in part-time jobs has occurred as a function of people seeking part-time work, such as mothers with young children who are joining or returning to the labour force (Barling, 1990), the effect of economic conditions on the increase of part-time jobs cannot be ignored as it has important implications. First, two important trends are evident from the data pertaining to the United States for the period 1968-93 (see Figure 3; Nardone, 1995): (1) involuntary part-time jobs increase far more rapidly during periods of recessions, presumably when individuals' options are more limited; and (2) ever since 1980, these increases in part-time jobs have been paralleled by *decreases* in the extent to which individuals are employed part-time on a voluntary basis. This phenomenon is replicated in Canada, as is evident from the data reflecting the pattern between 1975 and 1993 (Logan, 1994; see Figure 4). Presumably, any increase in involuntary part-time employment is linked to the declining availability of full-time positions (Noreau, 1994), and is not simply a function of individuals choosing to work part-time. The implications of individuals being forced to assume working arrangements that do not match their desired state will be considered later in this chapter.

FIGURE 2

INCREASE IN PART-TIME JOBS IN CANADA
BETWEEN 1975 AND 1993

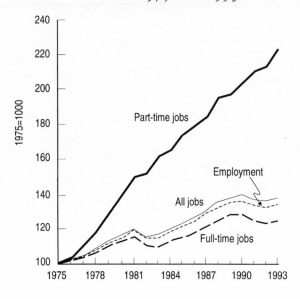

FIGURE 3

INCREASES IN VOLUNTARY AND NON-VOLUNTARY
PART-TIME WORK IN THE U.S., 1968-93

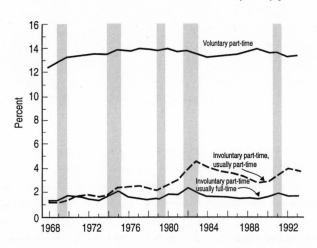

FIGURE 4

INCREASES IN VOLUNTARY AND NON-VOLUNTARY
PART-TIME WORK IN CANADA, 1975-93

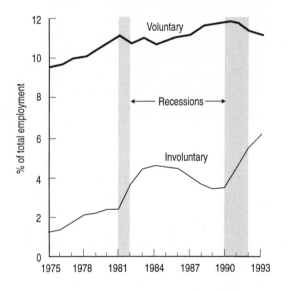

It is worth noting at this stage that providing realistic estimates of the extent of part-time work would be difficult. In Canada, any person working more than 30 hours per week is classified as a full-time employee (Pold, 1994); in the United States, the criterion is 35 hours (Gardner, 1996). Thus, in Canada, an individual working two part-time jobs for 20 hours per week each would be officially classified as a full-time employee. The reported number of individuals holding part-time jobs underestimates the real number, with this underestimate being greater in Canada than in the United States. This phenomenon may have critical implications, as policy makers, employers, unions and academics would be moved to action more readily if the real extent of the problem were realized.

The extent to which growth in part-time employment is a function of economic conditions (as opposed to individual volition) can be appreciated further from the differential growth rates in part-time and full-time work in Canada between 1975 and 1993. The proportion of full-time job creation is greatest in those provinces enjoying the most favourable economic conditions — British Columbia and Alberta.

In contrast, in provinces experiencing more challenging economic conditions — Newfoundland, Nova Scotia, Quebec, Manitoba and Saskatchewan — new job creation is limited almost entirely to part-time jobs.

One aspect of part-time work that is frequently overlooked is "moonlighting," which typically refers to any additional work engaged in by someone who has a full-time job. This phenomenon increased dramatically in Canada between 1977 and 1993 across all industries (Cohen, 1994; Pold, 1995). The amount of moonlighting is also relatively substantial: the vast majority of moonlighters holding a full-time job in Canada are also engaged in their second job every week (usually one or two days per week). On average, men moonlight approximately 14 hours per week, and women about 11 hours. Moonlighting is important for at least two reasons. First, the actual number of part-time jobs in the economy (as opposed to the number of people working on a part-time basis as defined above) is vastly underestimated. Second, the single most frequent reason given for engaging in moonlighting is financial. One-third of moonlighters do so because it is the only way to meet their regular household expenses; an additional 29 percent do so because they are saving for some specific item or event, or paying off a debt (Cohen, 1994).

Clearly, therefore, many individuals are not engaging in part-time work by choice. This is critical as research shows that when employed mothers' employment status is not consistent with what they want (e.g., full-time employees who want to be employed on a part-time basis, and part-time employees who want to be employed on a full-time basis), they score higher in terms of depression (Hock and DeMeis, 1990), and their children manifest more behavioural problems (Barling, Fullagar and Marchl-Dingel, 1987).

Self-Employment

Coinciding with ever-increasing levels of unemployment (see next section), there has been a marked growth in self-employment. An examination of the trends between 1981 and 1991 illustrates this growth in self-employment (Crompton, 1993). Excluding the agricultural sector (where there was a slight decline in self-employment from 2.2 percent to 1.8 percent of the experienced labour force), self-employment increased from 6.9 percent in 1981, to 7.5 percent in 1986, to 8.1 percent in 1991 of the total experienced labour force

(Gardner, 1995). Stated somewhat differently, while total employment grew by just over 14 percent in Canada between 1981 and 1990, self-employment grew by 29 percent during that same period (Pold, 1991).

In an era of chronically high unemployment, this movement toward self-employment emphasizing individual responsibility has become the mantra of many politicians. However, major changes are involved when moving to self-employment (such as loss of benefits), not least of which is an increase in the number of hours worked. For example, while employees work on average 37.2 hours per week, self-employed independent workers work on average 39.7 hours per week, and self-employed employers average 47.1 hours per week (Gardner, 1995). One effect of the lack of benefits to the self-employed is that self-employed individuals are more likely to work later in life. To illustrate this point, we note that between 17 and 18 percent of self-employed individuals remain working after the age of 55. In contrast, less than 10 percent of employees do so (Gardner, 1995).

Unemployment

Several interrelated factors concerning unemployment in Canada combine to make the idea of changing employment relations anything but attractive to employees. First and foremost, the national unemployment rate has increased over the past few decades. However, when workers look around themselves, they also see several other related factors that would no doubt cause them even more concern. For example, the average duration of unemployment has also been increasing (Cohen, 1991; Corak, 1993). Add to this the fact that following unemployment, most employees will assume a full-time or part-time job that pays less than their former job. Using U.S. data, Cappelli, *et al.* (1977) show, for example, that following a spell of unemployment, only 27.4 percent will be employed full-time with the same income or higher than the job they previously held.

These experiences, however, would not be felt uniformly; instead, there are marked variations in unemployment levels on a regional and an urban/rural level. Thus, the national unemployment rate does not provide an appropriate reflection of the extent of the problem, a factor that has been known for some time (see George Orwell's [1937] *The Road to Wigan Pier*). Similarly, there are distinct disparities in the duration of unemployment, with individuals being rehired off the unemployment roll with what Corak (1993) has described as a "last in, first out" phenomenon. Thus, concerns about a growing polarization within the work force are heightened, and we will return to this issue.

CHANGES IN THE QUALITY OF WORK

Perhaps the major reason that any changes in the amount, timing and availability of work are of some consequence is that they have an impact on the experienced quality of work. This section, therefore, examines how the subjective experience of work has changed consistent with transformations in employment relations.

The Quality of Work during the 20th Century

If a history of management were to be written by employees, what we would discover is that for most of the 20th century, the quality of work seemed to be increasing most of the time for most employees: while the number of hours decreased substantially, the quality of work improved dramatically. A brief examination of some of the historical turning points in the field of management and organizational behaviour during the 20th century will exemplify how this affected the quality of working life for most employees. It should be noted that this historical discussion provides a very brief overview of the development of the quality of work; for a more comprehensive picture, see Ott (1989).

From the perspective of the quality of work, the century got off to a bad start. By taking so much of the responsibility for work away from employees themselves, and handing it over to a group later to become known as industrial engineers (Taylor, 1911), Taylor's scientific management committed the cardinal error of separating the "doing" of work from the "thinking about" work. Following the now-famous Hawthorne study, however, there was a growing realization that social and group factors were critical in employee motivation, a notion that was later reinforced by findings from the Tavistock Coal Mining Studies.

Equally important in challenging the mechanistic notions of scientific management was Maslow's (1943) emphasis on self-actualization as the pinnacle of motivation. While Maslow's (1943) earlier writings were not intended for an industrial audience, Maslow can be credited with starting the process of bringing the role of individual needs back into the organization. This perspective was continued by Herzberg (1959), whose primary contribution was his introduction of the job enrichment approach.

Aside from these developments, perhaps the single most important influence was the establishment of the Institute for Social Research at the University of Michigan in 1947 by Rensis Likert. Together with many of the luminaries who were attracted to the institute (including Arnold Tannenbaum, Daniel Katz, and Robert Kahn), the ideas of employee participation in decision making and employee autonomy were popularized and tested at the Institute for Social Research. In this way, many of the excesses of scientific management began to be reversed, and this trend toward improvements in the quality of work life was accelerated by the growing realization of the importance of work-related stress (Kahn, *et al.*, 1964), and relational issues in leadership (McGregor, 1960).

Continuing with a historical analysis from the eyes of employees, we would find that starting in the mid-1980s, and accelerating thereafter, there was a reduction in the quality of work for most employees, as is evident from the following statement based on data from the United States Bureau for Labor Statistics:

Nearly half of America's businesses reduced their workforce during the last decade.... Today, companies routinely ask one employee to do the work of 1.3 people ... overtime is at an all time high, an average of 4.3 hours per week ... in the last decade, average yearly vacation and paid absence decreased by 3.5 days (Hancock, *et al.*, 1995).

Further illustrative of this dramatic reversal, 34 percent of people interviewed even more recently in a random poll in the United States indicated that they or someone in their families were moonlighting during the past three years, and 54 percent had to work overtime (*New York Times*, 1996). Nor were employees in Canada exempt from this turnaround, as is evident from a survey conducted in December 1995: 65 percent of employed respondents in a national representative sample indicated that they were now working more than they had a few years before, and only 16 percent of this group received an increase in pay consistent with their extra work (Angus Reid Group, 1995). Thus, regardless of any jargon about a "jobless recovery," most employees find themselves engaged in a "new, ruthless economy" (Head, 1996).

The "Age of Insecurity"

In trying to understand how most employees presently experience their work, the words of Robert Reich, former U.S. Secretary of Labor, loom large; he suggested that we are now in an "age of insecurity," one in which chronic uncertainty for employees is quite possibly the norm. With unemployment in Canada remaining at such high levels, and no real chance for a "job-full recovery" in sight, employees (or in the current jargon, "survivors") look around and are confronted everywhere with the remnants of organizational downsizing. Not surprisingly, therefore, job insecurity seems to be at an all-time high, and together with the increasing overtime work for many, job insecurity is probably the central concern of employed workers today (Canadian Auto Workers, 1997).

Why are employees so afraid of losing their jobs? Aside from the continuing number of people who are still being laid off, employees look around and see that the duration of unemployment is increasing, and that social and financial benefits for unemployed individuals in Canada are shrinking. Just as important, employees fear that losing a full-time job may mean assuming one or more part-time jobs. And it is not just the diminution of hours, and even salary, which often follows layoffs, that casts fear into employees. One factor that has increased substantially over the past 50 years is the level of benefits received by full-time employees: while benefits were just over 15 percent of regular salary in 1955, by 1987 average benefits for full-time workers in Canada were approximately 35 percent of salary. Given that most part-time employees receive few, if any benefits, the prospect of losing one's job becomes even more scary. At the same time, it should be noted that even keeping one's job will be associated with having to work harder, probably for the same pay, and with lingering job insecurity.

Together with job insecurity come several associated feelings that reflect the massive changes in employment relations, namely, violated psychological contracts between employer and employee, and a feeling of loss of control. Aside from any legally binding contract between employee and employer, the implicit psychological contract has always served as a point of potential motivation or frustration for employees (Rousseau, 1995). Given that one of the most basic elements of this psychological contract has traditionally been one of job security in exchange for a reasonable quantity and quality of work, it is not surprising that feelings that the psychological contract have been violated are widespread. The possible consequences for organizations range from employee theft (Greenberg and Barling, 1996) to psychological and physical violence against authority figures in the workplace (Barling, 1996), and should serve as a sufficient cause for considering alternatives to layoffs and strategies that result in chronic job insecurity.

Perhaps the psychological experience that forms the foundation of job insecurity is a feeling of powerlessness (Ashford, Lee and Bobko, 1989); powerlessness to be able to exert any control over the most basic element of one's job. From a psychological perspective, this powerlessness reflects more than a feeling of lack of control. Because of the belief that one could previously control one's job security, the feeling of powerlessness reflects a feeling of a *loss* of control, which is more psychologically harmful than a lack of control. Nevertheless, feelings of powerlessness are associated with health-related problems, and employees who perceive some form of workplace control are less likely to respond to job insecurity with health problems (Barling and Kelloway, 1996). Similarly, employees who feel a lack of control also tend to be less productive and less satisfied (Stanton and Barnes-Farrell, 1996).

UNINTENDED CONSEQUENCES OF CHANGING EMPLOYMENT RELATIONS

We have long known that children's knowledge about, and attitudes toward, the world of work are profoundly affected by their observations of their employed parents (Barling, 1990, 1992). If this is indeed the case, we need to ask what children might be learning as they see their parents experiencing layoffs and chronic job insecurity (Barling and Sorensen, 1997). Data now being accumulated suggests that when adolescents perceive their parents to be insecure in their jobs, their own work attitudes and work motivation (e.g., work-related cynicism) are negatively affected (Barling, DuPre and Hepburn, 1998). A separate study has shown that when adolescent university students see their parents' insecure about their jobs, their concentration is affected, resulting in poorer grade performance (Barling, Zacharatos and Hepburn, 1997). Thus, because experiencing job insecurity influences not just the individual job holder, but family members as well, greater attention should be given to the possible effects of changing employment relations.

PRODUCTIVITY AND PROFITABILITY

From a perspective that looks only at individual productivity and organizational profitability, the new changing employment relationship would be constructive if intended economic benefits were achieved, or at worst, if there were no negative effects. To the contrary, research findings are beginning to accumulate that suggest that the initial aims of the changes (to become "lean and mean") have not been realized; moreover, there are often negative effects. This is evident in at least three different levels — individual productivity, health and safety, and corporate profitability.

One criterion of individual productivity is innovation and problem solving, behaviours that are increasingly critical to success in today's business environment. Given this, it is of considerable importance that Dougherty and Bowman (1995) showed that problem solving is *lower* among employees in high-downsizing firms than their counterparts in low-downsizing firms, possibly because of a breakdown in networking in the destabilized, high-downsizing firms. These results are consistent with surveys showing that many of the anticipated benefits, such as better communications, do not materialize following downsizing (Cascio, 1993).

Moving to a consideration of occupational health and safety, Little, *et al.* (1990) demonstrated that corporate instability is associated with psychological stress and depression, and they question the long-term effects for employee and public safety. Kochan, Smith, Wells and Rebitzer (1994) extend this: while acknowledging that the use of temporary and contingent workers offers employers a high degree of flexibility required to meet rapid changes in labour demand, they found more workplace safety problems exist with contingent workers than with full-time workers. One possible cause of this is that employers are less likely to spend money on training individuals whose tenure with the organization is either very short or uncertain.

From an organizational perspective, the most profound questions concerning the viability of the new employment relationship derive from findings concerning post-layoff profitability. Cascio (1993) provided an early indication from survey data that intended economic benefits (reduced expense ratios, increased return-on-investments) do not necessarily emerge. Using case studies, Pfeffer (1994, 1998) takes a complementary but different approach, showing that offering some form of employment security can serve as a source of sustained competitive advantage, as has been the case at Lincoln Electric; and employment security is now an integral part of most conceptualizations of successful human resource systems (Pfeffer, 1998). Importantly, these observations are now supported by empirical data: based on a five-year study of the layoff histories of Fortune 500 companies, De Meuse, Vanderheiden and Bergmann (1994) showed that financial performance (specifically, profit margin, return on assets and return on equity) is worsened during the two years following layoffs. If the leading corporations in the United States, with all the resources available to them, cannot benefit from downsizing, we must ask ourselves how likely it is that less resourced or smaller organizations will benefit from similar strategies.

POLICY OPTIONS

The magnitude of the changes that have taken place cannot be underestimated. Then U.S. Secretary of Labor Robert Reich's observation that we are beginning to witness the "apartheidization" of the American workforce may not only be more true today (Freeman, 1996), but given the data presented above, is equally true of Canadian workplaces. However, even given the widespread changes that have taken place, and the effects they have wrought on the subjective quality of work, the purpose of this chapter is not simply to bemoan our collective fate. The more urgent need is to turn our attention to policy options that should be considered by employers, government, unions and academics. As Freeman (1996) suggests in concluding his article about the problems experienced as a function of changing employment relations, "Let's start reasoning together about how to solve them" (121).

Government

Consistent with (1) a tilt toward more right-wing governments in North America that started in the 1980s; (2) the corporatist refrain from the business community for ever-decreasing levels of government intervention in business; and (3) the fall of communism in the former Soviet bloc, perhaps the most basic question confronting government is whether it has any legitimate role in changing employment relations at all. Like Charles Handy (1995), however, I would argue that while the old order has undoubtedly changed, it simply does not follow logically that everything in the old order was necessarily bad. As Handy (1995) concluded "The end of communism does not mean that capitalism, in its old form, is therefore the one right way" (270), and it is premature to throw the baby out with the bathwater. Mintzberg (1976,

75) reaches the same conclusion from a different perspective, that it would be inappropriate to move from one extreme model to another. He observes that: "'Capitalism has triumphed.' That was the pat conclusion reached in the West as, one by one, the Communist regimes of Eastern Europe began to fall.... Capitalism did not triumph at all; balance did.... The countries under communism were totally out of balance." Mintzberg (1976, 75) continues, reminding us that "When the enterprises are really free, the people are not." Thus, consistent with the notion that government does indeed have a role in ensuring that a balance is maintained between the needs of business and the citizenry, several policy options might be considered, such as compulsory part-time benefits for part-time workers, placing a mandatory limit on overtime work, and the feasibility of employment models resulting in employment security.

One of the most profound of the changes in employees' experience of the world of work has been the extent to which traditional benefits may no longer be available; indeed, this may be one of the factors that make part-time jobs so attractive to employers. The notion of compulsory part-time benefits commensurate with the amount of part-time work may not be far-fetched; some form of this arrangement has been mandatory in Saskatchewan since 1995, and in the European Union as well. Even in jurisdictions where part-time benefits are not mandatory, more progressive private organizations (e.g., UPS, Starbucks) are implementing some benefits for part-time work, such as stock ownership, as an instrument of competitive advantage.

In Canada, unemployment is at an all-time high, as are levels of overtime work. The extent to which these two phenomena are related, and their consequences, should be confronted. As noted earlier, some employees are working more and more hours, and others find themselves with much less work than they would like. Various groups (such as the Canadian Labour Congress, and the Advisory Group on Working Time and the Distribution of Work, established by the federal government and comprised of business and labour leaders and academics) have called on the federal government to limit the amount of overtime work. To date, however, no action has been taken. At the same time, some provincial governments, like Ontario, are proceeding with plans to *increase* the amount of overtime work employers can ask employees to engage in, to limit employees' right to refuse the overtime, and to extend the definition of normal hours beyond that of 48 hours per week, thereby limiting the amount workers would get paid for doing even more work.

Why do employers oppose any limits to the amount of overtime allowed? Perhaps the most salient factor is the legislated structure of compensation: it is more profitable for employers to ask 40 employees to each work an extra hour than to hire one more worker for 40 hours, because benefits paid to workers, and the various taxes paid to governments, are based on the number of employees, rather than on the number of hours worked. Government has a role in ensuring a balance between the needs of employers and employees; however, they are by no means simply an interested bystander. There is a potential conflict of interest as any change in the legislation would result in governments themselves having less access to employees working overtime as well, precisely when shrinking budgets and fighting deficits is their self-imposed primary aim. Until some modification occurs in the legislation governing compensation and hours worked, however, little change can be expected.

Following closely on the heels of the private sector, governments across North America joined the rush toward downsizing. The consequences of this for productivity will be discussed in terms of policy options for employers; what is at stake here is the broader social consequences of widespread unemployment and chronic job insecurity. The medical, social and familial costs of unemployment have long been known (Barling 1990; Jahoda, 1982; Warr, 1987). What is becoming increasingly evident is that chronic job insecurity is associated with equally negative effects. Given this, government's role is to ensure a balance between the needs of the corporate world on the one hand, and the mental and physical well-being of the citizenry on the other. Following from Mintzberg's (1996) argument concerning the importance of balance, government's role must be to ensure that the needs of corporations are not fulfilled at the expense of the citizenry.

Employers

Charles Handy (1995, 9) tells the story of two junior executives bemoaning their excessive work involvement, one of whom ended the discussion by stating: "It's a crazy system. It doesn't make sense. Why don't they employ twice as many people at half the salary and work them half as hard? That way they could all lead a normal life." However, Handy (1995) holds out no hope that this might happen anytime soon, given the central belief that dominates and drives changing employment relations — that productivity and profit can be summarized as "1/2 x 2 x 3 = P," i.e., half as many people, all of whom are paid twice as much, producing three times as much, will result in increased productivity and profitability.

In sharp contrast to this belief, however, data being accumulated suggest that this model of employment does not necessarily result in higher levels of employee performance (e.g., Cascio, 1993; Dougherty and Bowman, 1995; De Meuse, Vanderheiden, and Bergmann, 1994). Instead, case studies of demonstrably and consistently successful organizations such as the Lincoln Electric Company show that some form of employment security (as opposed to job security) is a critical element in producing sustained levels of high-quality employee performance, which can serve as a competitive advantage (Pfeffer, 1994, 1998). In addition, controlled empirical studies show that mentally and physically healthy employees involved in jobs that are interesting and challenging result in higher levels of work performance (e.g., Wall, *et al.*, 1990).

As a result, while acknowledging that full job security is not feasible within a market economy, it behooves management to examine alternative models that stand a better chance of achieving their aim of ensuring higher levels of employee performance. In the process, revisiting fads such as re-engineering would be worthwhile given current concerns about its success (Byrne, 1997). This is critical, given that the available data, rather than management fads, suggest that a more plausible alternative to Handy's formula would read: ".7 x 1.3 x 1 x ↓B≠P," i.e., that 70 percent of the people working 30 percent more hours for the same pay while receiving fewer benefits will never be more productive!

Unions

Changes in employment relations over the past 15 years have presented major challenges to organized labour, so much so that some observers have concluded that organized labour is finally obsolete and irrelevant. At the same time, however, I would argue that depending on how unions respond, changes in the quantity, availability and quality of work may paradoxically present the labor movement with its greatest opportunity in recent times. Several challenges, however, will need to be overcome, including organizing part-time workers and influencing legislation.

Unions have traditionally paid less attention to, and have been less successful in organizing part-time workers in an economy that emphasized full-time jobs (Barling, Fullagar and Kelloway, 1992; Barling and Gallagher, 1996; Kelloway, Barling and Harvey, 1998). With the recent and continuing growth in part-time jobs both in absolute terms as well as relative to the total number of jobs, unions will continue to ignore part-time employees at their own peril. Paradoxically, one reason why unions have been less than enthusiastic about organizing the part-time sector is their belief that the growth in part-time work really reflects a management attempt to avoid, or even decertify unions. Yet this is perhaps the very reason for unions to pursue aggressively attempts to organize part-time workers.

What unions do not win through collective bargaining they often pursue through legislative change via political lobbying, and vice versa. Recent legislative endeavours in many jurisdictions across Canada can at best be seen as an attack on the power, if not the very existence, of the union movement. Whether governments are overturning existing bans on replacement workers, or reducing the right to strike among certain workers in Ontario, or intervening in union-management issues, such as the confrontation between the Canadian Auto Workers and Canadian Airlines at the end of 1996, unions see their power potentially eroding. The extent to which unions can achieve gains in legislation will be critical to their overall success: consistent with the model of "business unionism" within which unions focus their attention on bread-and-butter issues, labor unions will attract new members and the continuing support of their current members to the extent to which they deliver valued outcomes (Barling *et al.*, 1992). Given that the challenges inherent in changing employment relations extend beyond any one workplace, workers may well look to their unions to gain some legislative relief through political lobbying and political action campaigns such as the Days of Protest in Ontario in 1996 against the Progressive Conservative government. These activities are widely recognized as a legitimate tactic for unions, and can certainly be effective (Catano and Kelloway, 1997). Simply stated, unions need to again demonstrate their effectiveness and utility both to their members as well as to workers in general, which includes both full-time and part-time employees.

Academics

Academic researchers have traditionally enjoyed the luxury of researching whatever issues took their fancy, communicating their results with relatively small groups of peers. A new challenge now confronts academics: what happens when our research findings teach us, as they do in the case of changing employment relations, that all may not be well, that productivity gains may not be achieved, and that workers may be hurting in the process? Given that this situation is occurring, I would argue that it is no longer acceptable for researchers to act as if they operate in a vacuum. We need to share our results with those people, whether management or workers, whose success and well-being might be changed with some of the knowledge that has recently been gained.

If this model is pursued, however, it would not be appropriate to simply share our results. Instead, a more productive course would be to conduct further research with those affected, rather than on those who are affected. This would mean involving all affected parties, including legislators, management and workers in setting the research agenda, and encouraging their participation in deciding the appropriate methodology for further research. While not underestimating the enormity of the change from current practice this would reflect, research on changing employment relations in particular, and our understanding of work in general, would become more relevant if this strategy were to be followed.

CONCLUSION

Given the preceding discussion, it would be redundant to reiterate that work has indeed changed. However, it would be worthwhile ending this chapter reiterating several truths. First, the recurring theme within all the changes in employment relations is the extent to which employees are losing opportunities to exert control over their work, their workplaces and their work lives. Yet, workers both feel better and do better when they believe they can exert control. Consequently, to ensure higher levels of employee performance and psychological well-being, an intensive examination of current employment relations, and in what direction they are headed, is urgently required. Second, it is obvious that organizations need to be more productive and profitable. It is equally obvious that psychological and physically healthy employees are in the best position to help their organizations achieve this aim. Focusing solely on higher levels of productivity in the short-term is no longer appropriate, and it now behooves governments, employers, unions and academics to simultaneously generate ways of ensuring the productive well-being of corporations and the psychological well-being of employees. Last, but by no means least, while work has changed dramatically, there is absolutely no indication whatsoever that work will become any less important psychologically to employees in the future. Instead, because of its role in ensuring that financial necessities can be met, and the role of employment in overall psychological well-being (Jahoda, 1982), work will remain central in our lives. Accordingly, government, management, workers, unions and academics need to intensify their focus on the meaning and consequences of changes in employment relations.

ACKNOWLEDGEMENTS

Financial assistance from the School of Business, Queen's University at Kingston, Ontario is gratefully acknowledged.

Statistics Canada information is used for Figures 1, 2 and 4 with the permission of the Minister of Industry, as Minister responsible for Statistics Canada. Information on the availability of the wide range of data from Statistics Canada can be obtained from Statistics Canada's Regional Offices, or from its World Wide Web site at http://www.statcan.ca or its toll-free access number 1-800-263-1136.

Figure 3 is reprinted with permission from the *Journal of Labor Research*.

REFERENCES

Angus Reid Group (December 26, 1995), *The Public's Agenda, Assessment of 1995, the Death of the Middle Class, and Charities/Luxuries* (Toronto: Angus Reid Group).

Ashford, S.J., C. Lee, and P. Bobko (1989), "Content, Causes and Consequences of Job Insecurity: A Theory-Based Measure and Substantive Test," *Academy of Management Journal*, vol. 32, no. 4, 803-29.

Barling, J. (1990), *Employment, Stress and Family Functioning* (New York: Wiley).

——— (1992), "Work and Family: In Search of the Missing Links," *Journal of Employee Assistance Research*, vol. 1, no. 2, 271-85.

——— (1996), "The Prediction, Experience and Consequences of Workplace Violence," in *Violence On the Job: Identifying Risks and Developing Solutions*, G.R. VandenBos and E.Q. Bulatao, eds. (Washington, DC: American Psychological Association), 29-49.

Barling, J., K.A. DuPre, and C.G. Hepburn (1998), "Effects of Parents' Job Insecurity on Children's Work Beliefs and Attitudes," *Journal of Applied Psychology*, vol . 83, no. 1, 112-18.

Barling, J., C. Fullagar, and E.K. Kelloway (1992), *The Union and its Members: A Psychological Approach* (New York: Oxford University Press).

Barling, J., C. Fullagar, and J. Marchl-Dingl (1987), "Employment Commitment as a Moderator of the Maternal Employment Status/Child Behaviour Relationship," *Journal of Organizational Behaviour*, vol. 9, no. 1, 113-22.

Barling, J., and D.G. Gallagher (1996), "Part-Time Employment," in *International Review of Industrial and Organizational Psychology*, C.L. Cooper and I.T. Robertson, eds. (New York: Wiley), vol. 11, 243-78.

Barling, J., and E.K. Kelloway (1996), "Job Insecurity and Health: The Moderating Role of Workplace Control," *Stress Medicine*, vol. 12, no. 4, 253-59.

Barling, J., and D. Sorensen (1997), "Work and Family: In Search of a Relevant Research Agenda," in *Creating Tomorrow's Organizations: A Handbook for Future Research in Organizational Behaviour*, S. Jackson and C.L. Cooper, eds. (New York: Wiley), 157-70.

Barling, J., A. Zacharatos, and C.G. Hepburn (1997), "Effects of Parents' Job Insecurity on Children's School Performance," revised manuscript submitted for publication, School of Business, Queen's University, Kingston, Ontario.

Byrne, J.A. (1997, June 23), "Management Theory — or Fad of the Month?" *Business Week*, 47.

Canadian Auto Workers (1996), *Working Conditions Study: Benchmarking Auto Assembly Plants* (Willowdale, Ontario: Canadian Auto Workers).

Cappelli, P., L. Bassi, H. Katz, D. Knoke, P. Osterman, and M. Useem (1977), *Change at Work* (New York: Oxford University Press).

Cascio, W.F. (1993), "Downsizing: What Do We Know? What Have We Learned?" *Academy of Management Executive*, vol. 7, no. 1, 95-104.

Catano, V., and E.K. Kelloway (1997), "Evaluating the Effectiveness of a Political Action Campaign by Union Members," in *The Future of Trade Unionism: International Perspectives on Emerging Union Structures*, M. Sverke, ed. (London: Avebury), 361-75.

Cohen, G.L. (1991), "Then and Now: The Changing Face of Unemployment," *Perspectives*, vol. 3, no. 1 (Spring), 37-45.

———— (1994), "Ever More Moonlighters," *Perspectives*, vol. 6, no. 3 (Autumn), 31-38.

Corak, M. (1993), "The Duration of Unemployment during Boom and Bust," *Canadian Economic Observer*, vol. 5, no. 3 (September 4) 1-4, 20.

Crompton, S. (1993), "The Renaissance of Self-Employment," *Perspectives*, vol. 5, no. 2 (Summer), 22-32.

De Meuse, K.P., P.A. Vanderheiden, and T.J. Bergmann (1994), "Announced Layoffs: Their Effect on Corporate Financial Performance," *Human Resource Management*, vol. 33, no. 4, 509-30.

Dougherty, D., and E.H. Bowman (1995), "The Effects of Organizational Downsizing on Product Innovation," *California Management Review*, vol. 37, no. 4, 28-44.

Freeman, R.B. (1996), "Toward an Apartheid Economy?" *Harvard Business Review*, vol. 74, no. 1, 114-23.

Gardner, A. (1995), *The Self-Employed* (Toronto: Prentice Hall).

Gardner, J. (1996), "Hidden Part-Timers: Full-Time Schedules, but Part-Time Jobs," *Monthly Labor Review*, vol. 119, no. 9, 43-44.

Greenberg, L., and J. Barling (1996), "Employee Theft," in *Trends in Organizational Behavior*, C.L. Cooper and D.M. Rousseau, eds. (London: Wiley), vol. 3, 49-64.

Handy, C. (1995), *The Empty Raincoat* (England: Arrow Books)

Hock, E., and D. DeMeis (1990), "Depression in Mothers of Infants: The Role of Maternal Employment," *Developmental Psychology*, vol. 26, no. 2, 285-91.

Jahoda, M. (1982), *Employment and Unemployment: A Social Psychological Analysis* (Cambridge: Cambridge University Press).

Kahn, R.L., D.M. Wolfe, R.P. Quinn, J.D. Snoek, and R.A. Rosenthal (1964), *Organizational Stress: Studies in Role Conflict and Ambiguity* (New York: Wiley).

Kelloway, E.K., J. Barling, and S. Harvey (1998), "Changing Employment Relations: What Can Unions Do?" *Canadian Psychology*, vol. 39, no. 1, 124-32.

Kochan, T.A., M. Smith, J.C. Wells, and J.B. Rebitzer (1994), "Human Resource Strategies and Contingent Workers: The Case of Safety and Health in the Petrochemical Industry," *Human Resource Management*, vol. 33, no. 1, 55-77.

Krahn, H. (1995), "Non-Standard Work on the Rise," *Perspectives*, vol. 7, no. 4 (Winter), 35-42.

Little, L.F., I.C. Gaffney, K.H. Rosen, and M.A. Bender (1990), "Corporate Instability is Related to Airline Pilots' Stress Symptoms," *Aviation, Space and Environmental Medicine*, vol. 61, no. 11, 977-82.

Logan, R. (1994), "Voluntary Part-Time Workers," *Perspectives*, vol. 6, no. 3 (Autumn), 18-24.

Marshall, K. (1994), "Getting There," *Perspectives*, vol. 6, no. 2 (Summer), 17-22.

Maslow, A.H. (1943), "A Theory of Human Motivation," *Psychological Review*, vol. 50, no. 3, 370-96.

McGregor, D.M. (1960), *The Human Side of Enterprise* (New York: McGraw Hill).

Mintzberg, H. (1996), "Managing Government, Governing Management," *Harvard Business Review*, vol. 74, no. 3, 75-83.

Nardone, T. (1995), "Part-Time Employment: Reasons, Demographics, and Trends," *Journal of Labor Research*, vol. 16, no. 3, 275-92.

New York Times (1996), *Special Report: The Downsizing of America* (New York: New York Times Books).

Noreau, N. (1994), "Involuntary Part-Timers," *Perspectives*, vol. 6, no. 3 (Autumn), 25-30.

Orwell, G. (1937), *The Road to Wigan Pier* (London: Harcourt Brace).

Ott, S.J., ed. (1989), *Classic Readings in Organizational Behavior* (Belmont, CA: Wadsworth).

Peters, T. (1988), "A World Turned Upside Down," *Academy of Management Executive*, vol. 1, no. 3, 231-241.

Pfeffer, J. (1994), *Competitive Advantage Through People: Unleashing the Power of the Workforce* (Cambridge, MA: Harvard Business School Press).

———— (1998), *The Human Equation: Building Profits by Putting People First* (Cambridge, MA: Harvard Business School Press).

Pold, H. (1991), "A Note on Self-Employment," *Perspectives*, vol. 3, no. 4 (Winter), 46.

———— (1994), "Jobs! Jobs! Jobs!" *Perspectives*, vol. 6, no. 3 (Autumn), 14-17.

———— (1995), "Families and Moonlighting," *Perspectives*, vol. 7, no. 2 (Summer), 7-8.

Rousseau, D.M. (1996), *Psychological Contracts in Organizations: Understanding Written and Unwritten Agreements* (Beverly Hills, CA: Sage Publications).

Schorr, J. (1993), *The Overworked American: The Unexpected Decline of Leisure* (New York: HarperCollins).

Sheridan, J., D. Sunter, and B. Diverty (1996), "The Changing Workweek: Trends in Weekly Hours of Work in Canada, 1976-1995," paper presented at the conference on "Changes in Working Time in Canada and the United States," organized by the Canadian Employment Research Forum, Ottawa, June 13-15, 1996.

Stanton, J.M., and J.L. Barnes-Farrell (1996), "Effects of Electronic Performance Monitoring on Personal Control, Task Satisfaction and Task Performance," *Journal of Applied Psychology*, vol. 81, no. 6, 738-45.

Sunter, D., and R. Morissette (1994), "The Hours People Work," *Perspectives*, vol. 6, no. 3 (Autumn), 8-13.

Taylor, F.W. (1911), *The Principles of Scientific Management* (New York: Harper).

Wall, T.D., M. Corbett, R. Martin, C.W. Clegg, and P.R. Jackson (1990), "Advanced Manufacturing Technology, Work Design and Performance: A Change Study," *Journal of Applied Psychology*, vol. 75, no. 6, 691-97.

Warr, P.B. (1987), *Work, Unemployment and Mental Health* (Oxford: Oxford University Press).

5

RURAL RETREAT: THE SOCIAL IMPACT OF RESTRUCTURING IN THREE ONTARIO COMMUNITIES

Belinda Leach and Anthony Winson

IN APRIL 1996 the *Kitchener-Waterloo Record* (April 9, 1996, 1-2) published a front-page article based on our research. The article faithfully reported the negative consequences suffered by many workers following plant closures in three rural communities within about 60 kilometres of Kitchener-Waterloo, and captured the pessimism we felt for the futures of rural communities that continue to place their faith in attracting a major industrial employer as a solution to local economic development problems. The response to this article by town councillors in one of the communities was swift. The Mayor's rebuttal to our points was picked up by the newspaper a few days later. Things had apparently improved vastly since our interviews with laid-off workers in the community in 1994. The town had quickly recovered from the blow of losing a major employer, and these more recent changes were not reflected in the article. In a follow-up article in the newspaper a week later (*Kitchener-Waterloo Record,* April 16, 1996) in which the Mayor identifies two manufacturing facilities that had located in the town since 1994, he is quoted as saying "[w]e more than made up for everything we lost." The original article was apparently on the agenda of the next meeting of the Town Council, to which we were not invited. We received phone calls from one town councillor registering the disapproval of Council, and, as he told us, of local real estate agents. During the conversation, he too, reported on the improvement in economic conditions in the town, noting as evidence of this that "a Tim Horton's [coffee and donut shop] opened here just last week."

The unhappy response of Town Council to the very public exposure of our academic research draws attention to a number of problems confronted by, on the one hand, social scientists attempting to put a human and local face on abstract processes of restructuring, and on the other, municipal policy makers attempting to deal with the increasingly thorny issues of economic development and community viability.

Since at least the 1960s, rural Ontario communities have been engaged in a struggle in two major areas affecting their economies. They have witnessed the decline of the agricultural base of their communities, as family farms have failed and farm land has been incorporated into larger, commercial farms requiring less labour (Hay, 1992). During the same period, locally owned and operated manufacturing firms, which have often provided secure and reliable off-farm employment, have been acquired by larger companies with head offices hundreds, sometimes thousands, of kilometres away. These trends have altered dramatically the relationship between local policy makers and the enterprises forming the economic base of their communities. As these remote companies restructure, as they have done through the 1980s and 1990s, local politicians are relatively powerless to affect decisions that will have important consequences for the future of their communities.

One of the remaining powers local policy makers do have is to enhance the image of their communities in the hope that that will help to attract economic resources. Thus, they attempt to make their community (in contrast to others, perhaps) appear vibrant, positive and future-oriented. Our decision to go public with the results and analysis of our research was clearly in conflict with their objectives.

Our overt objective was a quite different one. As engaged social scientists, observing with critical awareness rather than simply documenting change, we wanted to reveal those social aspects of restructuring frequently overlooked by analysts of macroeconomic processes and policy makers alike. It seemed to us that most analyses of corporate and state restructuring paid rather perfunctory attention to the consequences of these processes for the people whose lives are affected, and for the communities in which they live. We wanted to investigate what happened when major employers "restructured" in three rural manufacturing-based Ontario communities in the early 1990s. What happened to the displaced workers and their families left to try to put their lives back together in a changed rural economy? Did local residents notice an impact on their community?

This paper continues our attempts to analyze what happened to those who lost their jobs, and to their families. In the first part, we examine the context that rural municipalities find themselves confronting, in terms of global economic restructuring and associated public policy changes, and the resulting trends in occupational structure and institutional infrastructure. We consider the particular implications of these shifts for rural manufacturing-based communities. In the second part, we present the findings of our study, looking first at the broad trends in wage rates and the kinds of job available. Then drawing on interviews with those caught up in the day-to-day effects of global processes, our research follows three families over a number of years as family members seek to replace the "good" jobs that were lost. We argue that the historical lack of attention to the rural implications of macroeconomic policies, now exacerbated by rapid restructuring, leaves individuals, families, communities and municipalities struggling to hold lives and livelihoods together. Our data suggest that for these particular communities, corporate strategies and state policy shifts shaping the new rural economy significantly reduce the chances of these workers finding comparable employment locally, thereby weakening the viability of the communities. Finally, we return to consider the role of local policy makers in restructured local economies.

THE POVERTY OF RURAL POLICY

In an assessment of federal rural development policy, Richard Phidd concludes that historically "one cannot find any significant commitment to rural development in terms of policies and programmes" (1994, 193). He argues that instead, federal attention to the rural areas has tended to flow from other policy fields, notably agriculture, but also forestry, conservation and recreation. This scattering of policy initiatives among several major federal government departments leads to one of the major problems facing communities at the policy level — the absence of an integrated approach to rural development. During the 1990s, there have been attempts to co-ordinate work in these areas, such as by the federal Ministry of Small Communities and Rural Areas, set up in 1993. Yet the fact that in his annual assessments of the rural scene in Canada from 1990 to 1993, Robert Dilley finds it necessary to include a section entitled "rural reorganization," which summarizes the many changes in bureaucratic responsibility at the federal and provincial levels from year to year (Dilley, 1994; and previous volumes from 1991), is highly suggestive of policy instability.

Within the more cohesive area of agricultural policy there have also been shifts that have led to disadvantages for rural communities.

The major policy tool through the 1960s and 1970s was the Agricultural and Rural Development Act (ARDA). Despite its apparent commitment to rural development per se, it has been criticized for bypassing the rural poor, and creating a situation in which rich farmers became richer and poor ones poorer (Lotz, 1977). Phidd (1992) argues that during this period, policy initiatives turned away from securing the future of the family farm toward a more general food policy. Lapping and Fuller (1985) reported that until the mid-1980s the stream of people leaving traditional family farming continued unchecked, as policy turned away from an agricultural focus toward regional economic development privileging urban centres. This policy focus has treated rural areas as residual, reinforcing inequality while providing little solution for rural poverty beyond encouraging the rural exodus even further.

The 1990s have seen the demise of regional development initiatives as part of the neo-liberal emphasis of a federal government intent on reducing the role of the state in society. Most notably this has included restructuring access to the national unemployment insurance program. This policy shift has had specific regional and rural impacts, disadvantaging marginal areas such as East coast fishing communities whose inhabitants had been regular benefactors of (and dependants of) unemployment insurance benefits due to the seasonal nature of economic activities in this region. Federal policy to restructure access to unemployment insurance funds coincided with the collapse of the federally managed cod fishery in Atlantic Canada, provoking a political crisis for the federal Liberal party in the Atlantic provinces during the 1997 election.

In a situation where "there have been few coherent policies for rural Canada since World War II" (Fuller, *et al.*, 1989, 3), it is hardly surprising that local municipalities have more recently placed their faith in attracting and keeping industrial enterprises to provide an economic engine for rural communities. For some communities this continues a long history of diversified manufacturing (see, for example, Parr, 1990), providing off-farm employment for some, and stable lifetime employment for other rural residents. The food processing plants in the communities described below fit into this category of long-standing industry with deep local roots. More recently, some rural communities have developed well-serviced industrial parks, hoping to attract "footloose" industry, that is industry not firmly tied to a particular location. One of the communities we examined, Mount Forest, had succeeded in doing this when Westinghouse made the decision to build a facility to produce electrical components there. This strategy continues today, with sometimes even greater zeal as recession and restructuring batter rural communities. Tiverton, Ontario, for example, opened an industrial park in 1992 to process farm products locally rather than having them shipped to urban centres (*Daily Commercial News*, July 14, 1992). Strategies such as these also hold out the promise of attracting an industrial plant, that would provide enough well-paid, secure jobs to have significant multiplier effects through the community.

RURAL RESTRUCTURING

The policy vacuum at the federal and provincial levels, which necessitates moves such as those outlined above, leaves rural areas vulnerable to the impact of policies developed within and about the urban context, as has occurred historically. In the last couple of decades, however, rural communities have become vulnerable to more than just urban Canadian decision making. When local policy makers adopt the industrial route — "smokestack chasing" as it is rather pejoratively termed — they become caught up in the web of financial and corporate manoeuvring that characterizes globalization. Thus, industrial employment in the community can be detrimentally affected by state policies and corporate strategies developed in many "elsewheres" and with entirely different objectives, paying little attention to the daily lives of the people affected by them.

Among the global policy shifts that affect rural communities seeking to expand or consolidate their industrial bases are those adopted to facilitate trade liberalization. While trade barriers between countries have been dismantled gradually over several decades, in the last few years the pace of such change has accelerated, especially recently with the rise of neo-liberalism and the election of governments committed to it. Neo-liberal policies promote freer trade and financial markets, and a reduction in government operations, thereby opening up and restructuring the economy. It is increasingly well accepted that these shifts are radically altering the structure of business enterprise, the organization of work, the quality of life on and off the job, and the role of the state in shaping these (Blackaby, 1979; Bluestone and Harrison, 1982; 1988; Morissette and Berube 1996).

Bluestone and Harrison (1982) posit a deindustrialization thesis, based on evidence of lost plants and jobs in the U.S. industrial heartland. They relate this to an increasing reliance on foreign assembly, outsourcing, co-production arrangements and licensing agreements with foreign competitors. This has been combined with corporate flexibility strategies to increase profits in the face of rising competition. These strategies include pressure on workers' overall compensation packages; a tiered workforce and wage structure; the use of contingent (part-time, contract, home-based) workers when possible; and attempts at union avoidance (Economic Council of Canada, 1990; Yalnizyan, *et al.*, 1994; Harrison, 1994), resulting in "occupational skidding" away from security and stability of employment, into contingency and uncertainty.

As the traditional industrial base has been eroded, there has been a concomitant rise in the service sector, which some argue will provide the latest engine for the economy (McKenzie 1985). Recent studies in the United States, Canada and elsewhere, however, demonstrate that service industries tend to be associated with low-wage jobs, disproportionately filled by women, immigrants and visible minority workers (Drache, 1991; Ross and Trachte, 1991; Menzies, 1996). Canadian evidence points to the high incidence of non-standard forms of work (part-time, contingent) in the service sector as partly responsible for the rise of new and disturbing inequalities in the wage structure (Economic Council of Canada, 1991; Morissette, 1995; Morissette and Berube, 1996; Yalnizyan, *et al.*, 1994).

A number of trends are associated with the rise of the service sector and the decline of manufacturing in Canada. The incidence of long-term unemployment has increased substantially over the 1980s (Gera, 1991), with Ontario witnessing by far the largest increase (Corak, 1993). This is in line with the situation in the United States (see Topel, 1993). Older workers have been particularly hard hit by some of the changes, most noticeably in finding new work to replace lost jobs (Gera, 1991; Corak, 1993). Women workers have also been noted as finding it more difficult to secure full-time jobs in the new economy (Armstrong, 1996). As well, corporate flexibility strategies creating more home-based and part-time jobs appear to be consistent with women's needs for flexible work arrangements associated with family care, yet they may be leading to new forms of gender inequality (Jenson, 1996; Leach, 1993; Leach, 1996).

These trends are occurring at a time when the state is retreating from its traditional role in the welfare of individuals and families, and programs are suffering from financial cutbacks. State programs are therefore least able to provide the traditional social safety net at precisely the time when they are most needed. As well, recent policies such as those that release patients into the care of the "community" soon after major surgery or trauma rather than keeping them hospitalized as in the past, or the cancellation of kindergarten programs leaving young children in need of all-day care, devised as cost-saving measures, place increased pressure on the workload at home, particularly for women. These kinds of policies make it increasingly difficult for women to take paid work outside the home, and this is happening at exactly the time when other effects of restructuring (such as job loss or instability) make additional income even more essential (Redclift and Whatmore, 1990).

Little has been written of the effects of restructuring on rural areas and small towns in Canada. Evidence from Europe and the United States indicates that some rural regions take on a new vibrancy as firms select rural locations in preference to urban ones (see Marsden, *et al.*, 1993; Saraceno, 1995). Sometimes the choice of a rural location is associated with the search for a compliant and docile labour force, without a history of militant labour struggle, in rural "greenfield sites." Other analysts argue that rural areas in the United States have been falling behind urban centres where better paid high-technology and financial services jobs tend to be located (Freshwater and Deavers, 1992). Fuller, *et al.* (1989, 14) argue that rural industries tend to involve "routine manufacturing," which is particularly vulnerable to competition from low-wage countries. Complex industrial plants, associated with more sophisticated technology, often electronic, and highly skilled jobs, tend to be disproportionately located in metropolitan regions, or when they are located in non-metropolitan regions are likely to provide less skilled jobs. Despite the fact that in theory new technologies are less locationally specific than some older ones (Fuller, *et al.*, 1989), this by no means ensures equal access to the fibreoptic lines required for high-technology services. Saskia Sassen (1995) has pointed out how urban places are not served equally by fibreoptic technology. She argues that the density of fibreoptic lines to areas of Los Angeles closely correlates with race and class divisions in the city. Similarly, rural areas are often not well served in comparison to urban centres. Moreover, access to fibreoptic lines does not ensure high-skill, well-paid, secure jobs, as the example of New Brunswick demonstrates (Buchanan and McFarland, 1997).

From her work in upstate New York, Fitchen (1993, 70) concludes that downsizing and the loss of rural manufacturing facilities have been largely responsible for the decline in rural employment, retail trade, and real estate values, and increased strain on community social services. The restructuring of state services is also particularly significant in rural areas that have been dependent historically on high levels of public spending associated with regional development, infrastructure support and agricultural subsidies (Marsden, *et al.*, 1993, 8).

As industry restructures, a new regional geography emerges, transforming previous locational advantages and disadvantages and restructuring local labour markets. These are now combining with new effects caused by changes in the role of the state. In the Canadian context, the decline in traditional manufacturing combined with the farm crisis of the 1980s and 1990s makes the rural situation particularly problematic (Winson, 1993; Leach and Winson, 1995). It is to an examination of these shifts and their consequences, in a particular local context, that we now turn.

WORKING AND NOT WORKING IN WELLINGTON COUNTY

Our study focuses on workers laid off from industrial plants in three communities in rural Wellington County, southern Ontario. The villages of Elora and Harriston and the town of Mount Forest were established as mill communities serving the surrounding farms. All have manufacturing histories dating back to the 1860s. Each has also exhibited considerable diversity in its manufacturing sector throughout this century, with firms coming and going and some managing to persist according to the vagaries of economic conditions. Located relatively close to the cities of Guelph and Kitchener-Waterloo, Elora is able to use this proximity to serve as a bedroom community. A poultry processing plant had existed there since 1962, and was acquired by Maple Leaf Mills in 1981, which was bought by Hillsdown Holdings PLC in 1987, and later merged with Canada Packers. When the plant closed in 1991, 130 people lost their jobs.

Harriston and Mount Forest are both about 60 kilometres from Guelph, a distance somewhat farther than an easy commute to the labour market in that city. The Canada Packers dairy plant in Harriston was the latest incarnation in a long-standing dairy history, dating back at least to 1900. Canada Packers had acquired the plant in 1927. When it closed in 1991, 101 people were laid off. The largest of the three communities, Mount Forest, also has a long history of manufacturing, although the Westinghouse electrical components plant had only located there in 1981. At the peak of its productive capacity, it employed 250 workers. Workers began to be laid off in October 1991, and the plant closed in July 1994.

The reasons for the plant closures are interesting. In the case of Westinghouse, the company's forays into speculative real estate deals during the 1980s, followed by the collapse of North American real estate markets at the end of the decade, led to massive losses including $2.7 billion in assets simply written off. The decision to restructure operations to cover bad loans forced the sale of corporate divisions and the layoffs of several thousand employees (Baker, *et al.*, 1992, 32-34). Canada Packers was bought by a British food processing giant, Hillsdown Holdings, which was interested in gaining access to North American markets, especially American ones made accessible through the Free Trade Agreement. Hillsdown sold off entire divisions of the company, and it quickly closed 20 plants including those in Elora and Harriston (Winson, 1993, 184-207). From these examples, it is clear that neither policy makers and unions nor local residents and workers could have prevented the plant closures. These were caused by factors largely unrelated to the local operations, and the decisions were made in the United States and Britain, far from Elora, Harriston and Mount Forest.

Working through key local individuals who had been involved in the unions at the closed plants, we sought laid-off workers from each of the plants to discover the subsequent trajectories of their work histories, and to compare the jobs they found with those they left. What follows is a summary of our quantitative findings, together with a closer look at the everyday struggles of three families. Our data consist of responses from 68 in-depth, face-to-face employee interviews. Several of these people also provided us with information about their spouses who had worked in the same plant.

In the summer of 1996, we went back to 34 of the 68 participants to find out how they had fared in the intervening two years, and were able to update our information on about 39 former plant workers. We interviewed them this time by telephone, asking a limited number of questions particularly related to their employment history since we had first interviewed them. Characteristics of people in the original sample are summarized in Table 2. We wished to analyze a number of characteristics of our sample group, including length of unemployment after layoff, type of job upon re-employment, quality of work issues, remuneration and economic well-being. We were concerned with the

TABLE 2

CHARACTERISTICS OF LAID-OFF PLANT WORKERS
(N=68)

	Canada Packers Harriston		Canada Packers Elora		Westinghouse Mount Forest	
Male/Female	10 / 12		3 / 13		13 / 17	
Median age	61	55	35	36	38	40
Unemployed	0	5	1	3**	3	3
Retired	5	1	0	0	0	1
Working long-term	5	6	2	8	10	13
Unemployment*	0	5	1	11	2	8

* Long-term unemployed = unemployment lasting one year or longer.
** Excludes two people in training programs.
Source: Interviews with plant workers, 1994.

gender dimensions of employees' experience after layoff, and how older workers had fared.

At the time of the initial interview in 1994, approximately one and a half to two years after layoff for most workers, fully 35 percent of our sample (24 of 68) were entirely without work. The majority of the unemployed (including those in training programs) were women (15 of 24). By the time of our reinterview in 1996, now at least four years after layoffs began, proportionately fewer people — 15 percent, or 6 of 39 — in the sample were unemployed, although by this time all those unemployed were women.

One of our more disturbing findings was that 61 percent of those interviewed in 1994 had spent at least a full year in unemployment. Of these long-term unemployed, the great majority were women (24 of 27). Of this unemployed group, seven (in 1994) were receiving pensions and considered themselves effectively retired, although most of them had told us they expected to work until 65. Closure of the plants forced some individuals to take involuntary early retirement, accompanied by lower pensions than they would have received had they worked until normal retirement age.

Age was another significant factor among those still unemployed at the time of interview in 1994. Of the 17 unemployed who were actively looking for work, 10 (58 percent) were over 50, while only 25 (37 percent) of the 68 in our overall sample were in that age bracket. Of those unemployed in 1996, only one was over 50.

At first glance, it might be easy to conclude that the unemployment situation improved markedly between our interviews with laid-

TABLE 3

PRE- AND POST-LAYOFF WAGES BY PLANT (C$)

	Canada Packers Harriston		Canada Packers Elora		Westinghouse Mount Forest	
	Men	Women	Men	Women	Men	Women
Pre-layoff (N=68) 1994	$11.77	$11.07	$12.00	$10.93	$14.90	$12.98
(N=68) 1996	$11.03	$ 9.18	$ 8.75	$ 7.90	$16.50	$ 8.29
(N=34)	$12.39	$ 8.62	$14.00	$11.19	$12.9	$10.22

Source: Interviews, 1994 and 1996.

off workers in 1994 and our contact with people again in 1996. This would support the position taken by Mount Forest Town Council members, who argued that the economic climate had improved considerably, and that there was no longer a significant problem related to the Westinghouse closure. In simple numerical terms this is correct, as the unemployment rate among the workers fell from 35 percent to 15 percent, although this remains well above the official unemployment rates for the province, which were 8.7 percent in 1995 and 9.1 percent in 1996 (Statistics Canada, 1997). Indeed, six of those interviewed who were working in 1996 had been unemployed when interviewed in 1994. A clue to the reality of the situation, however, lies in the fact that four of the six unemployed people in 1996 had only recently been laid off. Looking more closely at individual work histories over the intervening period, it becomes clear that for many workers periods of layoff followed sometimes by recall, sometimes by a new job, were a familiar pattern, so that the actual number of employed and unemployed fluctuated widely from month to month.

While the economic well-being of working people after layoff is clearly linked to length of unemployment, it is also determined by job characteristics upon re-employment. Overall, a comparison between wages received before and after layoff does not reveal a dramatic change, although wages tended to be lower overall on re-employment, with women faring less well than men (see Table 3).

The direct impact of these plant closures upon workers and their families becomes clearer when we examine changes in annual income, rather than hourly wages. Of the 19 women working in 1994, only one had experienced an income rise, while 16 had experienced a drop in income of at least $11,000. Five of the 15 men had experienced an annual income raise in their new jobs, but even here the circumstances were less than satisfactory. One was receiving more money because he now had to work six days per week instead of five. Two others reported that the additional costs of a long commute ate up most of their raise in pay. Of the remaining ten, eight had lost a minimum of $6,000 per year, while the other two were coping with the loss of more than $16,000 per year.

By the time of our reinterview in 1996, the annual income differential by gender was even more marked. Only two of 24 women were making more than their pre-layoff wage, and 15 were making at least $10,000 less. Among men, five of the 13 were making more annually than before they were laid off, in a couple of cases, more than $10,000 a year more, but the remainder reported a drop in yearly income. Overall, the average decline in income among respondents reinterviewed four years after layoff was 30 percent. It is noteworthy that this magnitude of income loss is in line with what some American studies of displaced workers have found (see Topel, 1993, 113).

A significant reason for the dramatic drop in annual income is that more and more of the jobs that are available are part-time, temporary contract or home-based jobs, rather than full-time, permanent jobs, supporting the observation that the contingent workforce is growing. In these casual jobs, workers are let go if the work drops off, to be picked up again if business improves. Thus, even minimal short-term job security is denied.

Of those who were working when interviewed, in 1994, 36 percent (two percent of the men and 54 percent of the women) were in part-time work, and in 1996, 57 percent (25 percent of the men and 78 percent of the women). The average hourly rate for part-time work compared to full-time work is shown in Table 4, and it is clear that the average wage of men took a dramatic drop when they accepted part-time work. For women in 1994, it was full-time replacement work that represented the largest hourly wage decline, and the difference between full-time and part-time was much less significant than for men. By 1996, however, the difference between average full-time and part-time wages had widened. It appears that this can be attributed to a polarization between those (few) women who are able to find full-time jobs at some distance from their communities of residence, and those who are compelled to accept part-time jobs locally, where part-time wages have been pushed downward between 1994 and 1996.

For many, working part-time means holding a number of jobs at one time in order to try to make up for the shortfall in income. Five of

TABLE 4

COMPARISON OF FULL-TIME AND PART-TIME WORK

	MEN				WOMEN			
	1994 (14)		1996 (12)		1994 (26)		1996 (18)	
	F-T	P-T	F-T	P-T	F-T	P-T	F-T	P-T
Total numbers	12	2	9	3	12	14	4	14
	(85%)	(15%)	(75%)	(25%)	(46%)	(54%)	(22%)	(78%)
Average hourly wage	$12.20	$8.85	$13.54	$10.85	$8.11	$8.82	$11.00	$7.05

Source: Interviews, 1994 and 1996.

the 16 people in part-time work in 1994 were juggling two or more part-time jobs to try to make ends meet. It is worth noting again that older workers fared differently from their younger co-workers. While eight of the 25 workers over 50 were in employment at the time of interview, six were in part-time jobs, and another was employed on a six-week contract.

It becomes clear from these data that the displaced workers in our study were not doing well even up to five years after layoff. To present a sense of how this affected the quality of both work and home life, and the connection between the two for these workers, it is useful to look at the experiences of three families. Identifying details have been changed to protect confidentiality. We do not intend these families to be taken as representative of the interviews as a whole, rather their individual stories demonstrate the kinds of situations that people confronted.

Sylvia and Fred

Fred had been employed at Westinghouse since it opened in the early 1980s, working as a welder. He was 51 when he received his layoff papers. When he was interviewed in 1994 he had been out of work for seven months, and was finding it difficult to find comparable work locally, although he knew there were opportunities further afield if he chose to commute. For some years since their children had left home, Sylvia had babysat children during the day. The Westinghouse layoffs affected her work too, since the parents of two of the children she cared for had lost their jobs as well. In spite of Fred's severance pay and unemployment insurance, even after seven months, they were beginning to feel the financial pinch. Since her mother lived close by, Sylvia was accustomed to being able to help her out financially in an informal way. Sylvia reported shopping far more carefully than she used to, and making less frequent trips to the shopping malls of Guelph and Kitchener-Waterloo. The couple had curtailed their routine of eating in a local restaurant once a week, Sylvia noting that this now meant she was cooking seven days a week. She also noted that "it's hurt everybody in Mount Forest," as merchants suffered a sales slump following the loss of Westinghouse pay cheques in the pockets of their customers. During their interview in early spring, they sadly considered the possibility that their planned driving vacation would have to be curtailed or even cancelled.

When we contacted Fred in 1996, he was working in Brantford (100 kilometres away), spending five days a week there, and coming home on the weekends. He said that under different circumstances they might consider moving, but not in this climate because "there's no guarantee the job would be there." The work was similar to his Westinghouse job, though he complained that his skills were not recognized, and although wages were better than before, the benefits package was much more limited. The new job was not unionized, and he had already run afoul of management by raising employment issues with them. He noted that when a pay raise was eventually granted, he was the only person who did not get one. Sylvia had found a job waitressing on weekends to supplement her unreliable income from babysitting.

John and Jessie

John and Jessie had both worked for Canada Packers in Harriston, John having 27 years seniority when he was laid off in 1991 at the age of 60. He had grown up in the area, worked on local farms as a young man, but when he and Jessie decided to get married he opted for a regular job in the town. During our interview in 1994, John talked about trying to come to terms with his inability to find a job following the plant closure. He had expected to work until he was 65, and felt he was "still too young" to retire. Two years later Jessie reported that John talked more easily about retirement. She too had found it difficult to find steady work following the layoff. She missed the job a lot, the people she socialized with were part of it, but of the work itself she said, "I loved it. But you have to move on, it's no good looking back." Just before we talked to her in 1994, she had taken full-time work at K-Brand, a sporting goods factory in Mount Forest, and was happy at the prospect of income. Their youngest child was finishing university, and she wanted to help him financially because the possibilities for summer employment for students in the area were very limited, even more so since Canada Packers had closed. She also reported her disappointment at being unable to provide the kind of family Christmas she used to for her children and grandchildren. By 1996 she had been laid off and called back several times by K-Brand, and had finally quit that job to pursue a home-based catering business. She said she was too old for full-time work.

Molly and Jeff

Molly and Jeff had both worked at the Canada Packers plant in Elora, where they had met. They were in their early 30s, with three small children at home, when they were both laid off. Molly quickly found work at a local supermarket. At first she worked 28 hours a week, then her hours were cut, first to 12 hours and then to five. At that point she quit the job, and decided to stay home with her younger children for a year. When we talked to her again in 1996, she was juggling working at the supermarket part-time with another part-time job in a nursing home. Jeff had managed to find a job in Stratford, about 70 kilometres from home. Molly reported that he was pleased that it was a unionized job, but disappointed to have to give up coaching Little League since, as he told her "once you get home you want to say there." Molly described the situation as very stressful because they had to juggle child care from one week to the next. As well, she said that the nursing home job was stressful in itself because every member of the part-time work-force was constantly fighting for more hours, and, she noted, this has been worsened by recent government cutbacks affecting the home.

THE SOCIAL IMPLICATIONS OF RESTRUCTURING

The evidence from these examples, and from many others, points to an overall decline in the quality of conditions on and off the job. Men were only better able than women to find equally skilled work if they paid the price for this by devoting many hours a week to a long commute. Women often told us their husbands would not consider the lower paid, less skilled jobs available locally. But for women, commuting to a more distant labour market was rarely a viable option. At first, this was because of children or other family responsibilities, and later, because male commuters monopolized the family car. Women were then limited to seeking work in the micro-labour market close to home, where the possibilities of work of any kind were scarce and for more skilled and better paid work practically non-existent. A number of women had managed to find full-time work at the K-Brand factory in Mount Forest, but Westinghouse workers wanting to keep working locally found their hourly wage drop from an average of $12.98 to $7.27 at K-Brand. They then faced layoff and recall parallel to the ups and downs of a firm operating in the competitive sector, a far cry from what some saw as the relatively secure market niche of a company like Westinghouse.

Most women, and some of the men, had found work in the service sector, where their hourly wage was low, often no more than minimum wage in restaurants and the retail sector. While the service sector in rural areas is overtaking other sectors in employment, it is not creating the better paid jobs in finance and high technology. Mount Forest had acquired new employers in the town. In late 1994, two companies announced that they were locating there. Vintex bought the old Westinghouse building in order to manufacture vinyl products. This company relocated from Mississauga, bringing all 60 employees with them (*Mount Forest Confederate*, October 4, 1994), and none of our respondents contacted in fall 1996 had been employed there. Long Manufacturing built a new plant in the town to make subcomponents for the auto industry, and two of our respondents had found work there.

The reality of working in non-union service sector and manufacturing jobs was becoming more and more evident to our respondents as they experienced it firsthand. One worker in a non-union job reported that co-workers had warned him that any discussion of wages among workers was viewed as grounds for dismissal. Pay raises were at the discretion (or whim) of management, and severance pay in the event of layoff (now accepted as a real possibility) was restricted to the minimum the law allowed. A major blow noted by most of the people we spoke to in 1996 was the loss of job-related benefits, such as extended health plans, dental plans, and life insurance. Even where these existed in new jobs, they tended to be less comprehensive than the plans workers had negotiated with their employers in their previous jobs.

In the context of public sector restructuring, these aspects of the new economy are significant. Workers who become unemployed now, as many of our respondents find themselves intermittently, are eligible for smaller unemployment insurance payments, covering a shorter period, and following a longer eligibility period. Welfare benefits, on which they may have to rely in the absence of a job when unemployment benefits have been exhausted, were cut back by 21.6 percent in 1995 by the Ontario Government. Because it is often less expensive to live in rural communities, some communities have witnessed an influx of welfare recipients from neighbouring cities following the cuts, leading to even greater competition for the available jobs. As well, transfer payment cuts affecting health services mean longer delays for medical procedures, and, perhaps more importantly, rural medical services are under review, with some hospital closures fairly certain to follow.

Older displaced workers face a relatively bleak future in rural areas as they compete with younger workers for jobs and find it more and more difficult to find work of any kind. Many of our respondents over 50 years of age were facing increasingly chronic health problems, without comprehensive extended health insurance, while the services they and their family members require, such as visiting nurses and home care, are diminishing.

CONCLUDING COMMENTS

A report in the *Sarnia Observer* in December 1996 describes how the village of Oil Springs, in southwestern Ontario, is struggling to maintain its identity and its social and economic base. Facing the closure of its bank, library and the nearby hospital, and the threat of amalgamation into the neighbouring township "small rural villages like Oil Springs are the end of the line for the restructuring decisions that roll down the tracks from Ontario's corporate boardrooms and cabinet meetings." The railway metaphor is curious. There has been no rail service to Oil Springs since the 1960s (*Sarnia Observer*, December 16, 1996, A3) when a previous round of restructuring had dramatic effects in the community. Mayor Byers of Oil Springs wondered, "what more are they going to take away from us?... It's just like we're constantly fighting a battle to preserve something."

A key question is what that "something" is, that Mayor Byers, and others in rural communities, are fighting to preserve. Mark Shucksmith has argued that the importance of the idea of rurality lies in its use as a symbolic shorthand for how people feel about and define rurality, and how these symbols are manipulated with "consequences for action and for the exercise of power" (Shucksmith, 1994, 127). He suggests:

"Different interests have tried to capture the definition of rurality to make their own conception the legitimate definition of rurality. Thus the definition of rurality is a site of social struggle within discourse, as promoters of competing representations strive for hegemony" (Shucksmith, 1994, 128). Shucksmith and his colleagues carried out research to determine whose interests the policy process concerning new rural housing development favoured (Shucksmith, 1994). While, as they expected, attitudes to the development issue matched class interests, it was only owner/occupiers who made sure they communicated their objections to planners and policy makers. Not one of the tenants, who supported the new development, had communicated this to policy makers. Local councillors were primarily influenced by owner/occupiers opposing the development, and by farmers who shared their background and their ideas about what rural actually means. Consequently, planning applications were denied unless they were submitted by farmers.

Within this kind of framework, the hostility on the part of local policy makers to our research findings becoming public is understandable. Town councillors usually come from the ranks of local business people whose interests are best served by an image of the rural town as thriving, positive and open for business. Our intervention into the discourse on a strategy for economic renewal was unwelcome since it introduced class dimensions by revealing the material reality for many displaced plant workers. This not only threatened the image of the town, it also suggested that the strategy adopted was not working for everyone, possibly raising councillors' fears for their own futures as policy makers.

The role for social scientists in exposing the contours of restructuring then becomes a political intervention in a dominant hegemonic discourse. Our contrary information is not only unwelcome, but we are also disadvantaged by the public's lack of understanding of how we do what we do. When our study findings were dealt with in the local press, the writer noted that "not one of those who gave the researchers information is identified, and it's also interesting to consider that they all had to be assured anonymity in order for them to talk." He also asked readers to consider whether "unidentified workers who have just been fired from their job, [are] the ones best qualified to say what happened and its effects on the community?" (*Mount Forest Olds*, April/May 1996, 3). As well as showing popular ignorance of the conventional social scientific practices of ensuring confidentiality and anonymity, these comments reveal an anti-working-class bias in the desire to individualize and identify, strategies long used by management to divide workers and break unions. More importantly for us, though, together with the Town Council's loud denouncements of our findings, they operate to diminish the significance of what working-class people have to say, to silence the voices our research sought to render audible.

Workers were first economically marginalized as a result of their job loss. Later they were politically marginalized as Council transparently refused to acknowledge their existence, and the local press questioned their right to contribute to the discourse. Meanwhile, some of our respondents told us (confidentially, of course) that they were impressed with the *Kitchener-Waterloo Record* article. If anything, the need for this kind of research, and its potential role in counter-hegemonic struggle, is only further reinforced.

REFERENCES

Armstrong, P. (1996), "Harmonizing Down in the New Economy," in *Rethinking Restructuring: Gender and Change in Canada*, I. Bakker, ed. (Toronto: University of Toronto Press), 29-54.

Baker, S., J.D. Dobrzynski, and M. Schroder (1992), "Westinghouse: More Pain Ahead," *Business Week*, December 7, 32-34.

Blackaby, F., ed. (1979), *Deindustrialization* (London: Heinemann Educational Books).

Bluestone, B., and B. Harrison (1982), *The Deindustrialization of America: Plant Closings, Community Abandonment, and the Dismantling of Basic Industries* (New York: Basic Books).

———— (1988), *The Great U-Turn: Corporate Restructuring and the Polarizing of America* (New York: Basic Books).

Buchanan, R., and J. McFarland (1997), "The Political Economy of New Brunswick's 'Call Centre' Industry: Old Wine in New Bottles," *Socialist Studies Bulletin*, no. 50, 17- 40.

Corak, M. (1993), *The Duration of Unemployment During Boom and Bust* (Ottawa: Statistics Canada, Analytical Studies Branch, no. 56).

Dilley, R. (1994), "Canada: The Rural Scene," in *Progress in Rural Policy and Planning*, A.W. Gilg, ed. (London: John Wiley), vol.4, 197-203.

Drache, D., and M.S. Gertler (1991), "The World Economy and the Nation-State: The New International Order," in *The New Era of Global Competition: State Policy and Market Power*, D. Drache and M. Gertler, eds. (Montreal: McGill-Queen's University Press), 3-25.

Economic Council of Canada (1990), *Good Jobs, Bad Jobs: Employment in the Service Economy* (Ottawa: Supply and Services Canada).

——— (1991), *Employment in the Service Economy* (Ottawa: Supply and Services Canada).

Fitchen, J. (1991), *Endangered Spaces, Enduring Places: Change, Identity and Survival in Rural America* (Boulder, CO: Westview).

Freshwater, D., and K. Deavers (1992), "Falling Farther Behind: Current Conditions in Rural America," in *Rural and Small Town Canada*, R. Bollman, ed. (Toronto: Thompson Educational Publishing), 45-67.

Fuller, T., P. Ehrensaft, and M. Gertler (1989), "Sustainable Rural Communities in Canada: Issues and Prospects," *Proceedings of the Agricultural and Rural Restructuring Group Conference* (Brandon, Man.), 1-41.

Gera, S. (1991), *Canadian Unemployment — Lessons from the 80s and Challenges for the 90s: A Compendium* (Ottawa: Economic Council of Canada).

Harrison, B. (1994), *Lean and Mean: The Changing Landscape of Corporate Power in the Age of Flexibility* (New York: Basic Books).

Hay, D.A. (1992) "Rural Canada in Transition: Trends and Developments," in *Rural Sociology in Canada*, D. Hay and G.S. Basran, eds. (Toronto: Oxford University Press).

Ip, G. (1996) "The Great Wage Divide," *Globe and Mail* (Toronto) October 26, 1996, B1.

Jenson, J. (1996), "Part-time Employment and Women: A Range of Strategies," in *Rethinking Restructuring: Gender and Change in Canada*, I. Bakker, ed. (Toronto: University of Toronto Press), 92-108.

Kitchener-Waterloo Record, April 9, 16, 1996.

Lapping M., and A. Fuller (1985), "Rural Development Policy in Canada: An Interpretation," *Community Development Journal*, vol. 20, no. 2, 114-19.

Leach, B. (1993), "Flexible Work, Precarious Future: Some Lessons from the Canadian Clothing Industry," *Canadian Review of Sociology and Anthropology*, vol. 30, no. 1, 64-82.

Leach, B. (1996), "Behind Closed Doors: Homework Policy and Lost Possibilities for Change," in *Rethinking Restructuring: Gender and Change in Canada*, I. Bakker, ed. (Toronto: University of Toronto Press), 203-16.

Leach, B., and A. Winson (1995), "Bringing 'Globalization' Down to Earth: Restructuring and Labour in Rural Communities," *Canadian Review of Sociology and Anthropology*, vol. 32, no. 3, 341-64.

Marsden, T., J. Murdoch, P. Lowe, R. Munton, and A. Flynn (1993), *Constructing the Countryside* (Boulder, CO: Westview).

McKenzie, R.B. (1985), *Competing Visions: The Political Conflict over America's Economic Future* (Washington, DC: Cato Institute).

Menzies, H. (1996), *Whose Brave New World?* (Toronto: Between the Lines).

Morissette, R. (1995), *Why Has Inequality in Weekly Earnings Increased in Canada?* (Ottawa: Statistics Canada, Analytical Studies Branch, no. 80).

Morissette, R., and C. Berube (1996), *Longitudinal Aspects of Earnings Inequality in Canada* (Ottawa: Statistics Canada, Analytical Studies Branch, no. 94).

Mount Forest Olds, April/May 1996.

Parr, J. (1990), *The Gender of Breadwinners* (Montreal: McGill-Queen's University Press).

Phidd, R. (1994), "The State and Rural Development in Canada," in *Towards Sustainable Rural Communities*, J. Bryden, ed. (Guelph: University of Guelph, School of Rural Planning and Development), 185-200.

Redclift, N., and Sarah W. (1990), "Household Consumption and Livelihood: Ideologies and Issues in Rural Research," in *Rural Restructuring: Global Processes and their Responses*, T. Marsden, P. Lowe, and S. Whatmore, eds. (London: David Fulton), 182-97.

Ross, R., and K. Trache (1991), *Global Capitalism: The New Leviathan* (Albany: State University of New York Press).

Saraceno, E. (1995), "The Changing Competitive Advantage of Rural Space," in *Progress in Rural Policy and Planning*, A.W. Gilig, ed. (London: John Wiley), vol. 5, 139- 54.

Sarnia Observer, December 1996.

Sassen, S. (1995), "Power and Marginality in Cyberspace," paper presented at the Annual Conference on Theory, Culture and Society, Berlin, August 10-14, 1995.

Shucksmith, M. (1994), "Conceptualizing Post-Industrial Rurality," in *Towards Sustainable Rural Communities*, J. Bryden, ed. (Guelph: University of Guelph, School of Rural Planning and Development), 125-32.

Statistics Canada (1997), "Statistical Summary," *Canadian Economic Observer*, July (Ottawa: Statistics Canada).

Tiverton *Daily Commercial News* (1992) "Rural Communities Hope to Attract Industry to Save Way of Life," vol. 65, no. 144, 9, 11.

Topel, R. (1993), "What Have We Learned from Empirical Studies of Employment and Turnover?" *American Economic Review*, vol. 83, no. 2, 110-15.

Winson, A. (1993), *The Intimate Commodity: Food and the Development of the Agro-Industrial Complex in Canada* (Toronto: Garamond Press).

Yalnizyan, A., T.R. Ide, and A.J. Cordell (1994), *Shifting Time: Social Policy and the Future of Work* (Toronto: Between the Lines).

6

IRON MEN, TRUE MEN, AND THE ART OF TREATY-MAKING

Olive Patricia Dickason

TREATIES AND ALLIANCES have been an important aspect of human affairs as long as people have lived in organized societies. This has been nowhere more evident than in the Americas, both before and after the arrival of Europeans, when numerous treaties were entered into for a wide variety of reasons. In pre-contact Canada, a principal function of these agreements was to stabilize relations between Aboriginal nations; in post-contact Canada, they were an important factor in controlling the spread of European settlement, and in ensuring its more or less peaceful character. Not only were these post-contact treaties of major importance when they were entered into, they are still in the forefront of Canadian/Amerindian politics, particularly in the prairie West, where the great land-cession treaties are woven into the Aboriginal social fabric. This is not to underrate the importance of earlier colonial treaties, such as those of the Maritimes and West Coast which, however, were more concerned with peace and trade, and Aboriginal acknowledgement of British suzerainty, than they were with land. Treaties as they evolved in Canada from the earliest period up to and including Treaty Eleven (1921), will be dealt with here, as well as the adhesions that continued well into the 1950s. After that there was a pause until 1975, when the James Bay Agreement was signed, followed by the Northeastern Quebec Agreement in 1978, and the Western Arctic (Invialuit) Claims Settlement in 1984. These later accords, while still concerned with land, place greater emphasis on political, economic, and social issues. They are outside the scope of this paper. In all, Canada has negotiated close to 500 treaties with its Aboriginal peoples.

In both European and Amerindian thought, treaties were based on natural law, which Cicero (126-43 B.C.) described as *non scripta sed nata lex* ("law that is not written, but born"), and Amerindians say "is given to us, not made by us" (The Indian Association of Alberta,

March 14, 1983). In both cases, it was conceived as a universal principle: to the Amerindians, it was an aspect of the universe as an interacting whole in which everything was interrelated; in their words, it "is only possible to understand something if we understand how it is connected to everything else" (Ross, 1996, 63-64). In the case of human beings, treaties were the means by which these connections were regulated between different groups, guided by natural law defined as a criterion of right conduct. Natural law was the principle of reasonableness that was promulgated in each man through his nature; whatever contradicted its principles was not binding. As Chief Mawedopenais put it on October 3, 1873, during negotiations for Treaty Three: "I will tell you what He [the Great Spirit] said to us when he planted us here; the rules that we should follow — us Indians — He has given us rules that we should follow to govern us rightly" (Morris, 1862, 59).

Europeans saw natural law as the forerunner of human rights, which preceded the formation of states. States, when they were formed, came within the orbit of natural law. This led to international law, which in today's terms is the consensus of the international community arising from the human will — that is, statutory law — rather than directly from natural law (Scott, 1934, 80). Another principle of natural law is the right of everyone to speak for themselves. The Romans had a legal maxim for that too: *quod omnes tangit, ab omnibus approbetur* (that which touches all is to be approved by all). It is known as the doctrine of consent. For Amerindians, this is still a basic principle, not only for treaty negotiations, but for public affairs generally. It involves reaching decisions by consensus, rather than by majority vote.

In the highly uncertain world of pre-Columbian hunters and gatherers, where strangers were likely to be considered enemies, it is almost impossible to exaggerate the importance of alliances and the treaties by which they were negotiated. Kinship and reciprocity were principal characteristics, and gift exchanges — "I give to you that you might give to me" — balanced the obligations incurred. Between First Nations, there could be agreement only if the gift exchange was equal. Rituals, often both extensive and elaborate, ceremonially sealed the commitments, which usually had social and political ramifications beyond the immediate purpose of the treaty. Thus, in 1619, Samuel de Champlain (c.1570-1635), having accepted overtures from the Huron and entered into a trading alliance with them, found that he was expected to march with his new allies against the enemy, in this case the Five Nations. If he had refused to do so, the alliance would have died even as it was being born.

THE FRENCH NEGOTIATE TRADE TREATIES

In the Americas of the 16th century, it was the French who pioneered friendship treaties with the Amerindians, their motivation being trade. Eyeing the stands of dyewood trees along the Brazilian coast (*Caesalpinia echinata* and related varieties, a source of red dye much in demand by the burgeoning European textile industry), they set about forging alliances with the native Tupi-Guarani, (particularly the Tupinamba, but also the Tamoio and Potiguar), even though the region was claimed by Portugal.[1] The French justified their actions by invoking the doctrine of consent, claiming that it gave all the peoples of the world, including Amerindians, the right to choose their trading partners.

In negotiating these alliances, the French were careful to follow Amerindian custom in order to give them validity in Aboriginal terms. Among other things, this meant that these agreements were not written, and that they had to be renewed from time to time with appropriate ceremonies and gift exchanges, as according to the Amerindian view they were subject to changing circumstances (Royal Commission on Aboriginal Peoples, 1995, vol. 2, Pt. 1, 11). (The idea that treaties were to endure as originally agreed upon "as long as the rivers flow and the grass grows" was introduced by 18th century White negotiators using Amerindian metaphor to express a European concept.[2]) Concerned that these arrangements also be recognized in Europe, the French took delegations of native Brazilians to France to be presented with great ceremony at the royal court, where they publicly asked for French protection as well as for missionaries to instruct them in Christianity. The French emphasized the point by staging baptismal spectaculars in which the highest nobles in France stood as godparents for the Amerindian converts. To Amerindians, baptism was part of the protocol that confirmed alliances, an approach that was in harmony with the pre-Reformation European attitude that baptism in effect conferred citizenship. In this way, the alliances were formalized from both Amerindian and European perspectives. Later, in Acadia, the baptism in 1610 of the paramount Mi'Kmaq chief Membertou (d.1611) and his family was commemorated in a wampum belt showing a priest standing below the Vatican symbol (crossed keys), holding hands with a Mi'Kmaq standing beneath a symbolic pipe and arrow. According to Mi'Kmaq oral tradition, this is the record of a "concordat" between their people and the Holy See. The French had another view: according to *Jesuit Relations*, the Mi'Kmaq had "accepted baptism as a sort of sacred pledge of friendship and alliance with the French," that being baptized made a Mi'Kmaq "almost a Norman."[3]

ROOM FOR MISUNDERSTANDING

As the above illustrates, there was plenty of room for misunderstanding in these early arrangements. Particularly when the stakes were high, which they usually were, there was too much opportunity for subtle plays on words, for twists in meanings and hidden agendas. For example, in 1671, the French, upset at the presence of the English on Hudson Bay, moved to outflank them by sending an expedition to the Great Lakes region. Ostensibly, it was to have "the name and the sovereignty of our invincible Monarch to be acknowledged by even the least known and the most remote Nations." This was a thinly veiled description of its actual purpose, which was to take possession of the interior of the continent, thus confining the English to the Bay. Fourteen First Nations were convoked to the Jesuit mission at Sault Ste. Marie, where the French combined a ceremony of possession with formal requests for permission to trade and for rights of passage through local territories (Perrot, c.1644-1717, 126-28, 292-94; Thwaites, 1896-1901, vol. 55, 105-15; Margry, 1976-86, vol. 1, 96-99). They told the assembly that they wanted "the fires of the Ojibwa and the French [to] be made one and everlasting" (Warren, 1984, 131).

The First Nations had no reason but to think that they had just gained a powerful new ally, one who would bring them desired trade goods and had promised to protect them from their enemies. The French considered that these new allies, by witnessing the ceremonial act of possession and by agreeing to accept French protection, had tacitly agreed to their assertion of sovereignty. Later, visiting Iroquois trading parties, more experienced in dealing with Europeans, tore down the French plaques of possession and took them to the English. The French, on learning this, knew that the Iroquois were aware that they (the French) had claimed the mid-West as theirs.

CONTINUING TRADITIONS

In New France, the fur trade, the economic life-blood of the colony, depended upon alliances. With the intensification of the French/English colonial wars, the military aspects of these accords moved to the forefront, and renewals became formalized in the form of annual ceremonial distributions of gifts to the First Nations in recognition of their military services to the French cause. The few occasions when the French entered into written treaties with Indians occurred when they were dealing with British allies, such as the Iroquois. The best known example of this was the 1701 peace treaty with the Five (later Six) Nations, signed in Montreal, formally ending the Iroquois-French wars that had been going on intermittently for a century.

The English preferred written treaties, perhaps because written documents more nearly reflected the permanence they expected of the agreements. It is clear from their texts that the British were using them as instruments to aid in their settlement and establishment of their suzerainty. The language was English; versions were not official-ly prepared in the appropriate Amerindian languages, even though interpreters had been essential for the negotiations. Participating Amer-indians signed with sketches of their totems, or with an X. The actual writing could be done by a scribe while the Indian delegate touched the pen.

For the First Nations, the treaties were ritualized compacts that established the reciprocal balance within which diplomatic and eco-nomic relations with Europeans could evolve in harmony (Friesen, 1986, 51); a written document merely symbolized the accord. Natives who were being confronted by growing tides of settlers and develop-ment projects came to view treaties as the most effective means available for protecting their interests. Such a procedure was sanctioned by tradition.

It is also clear that the basic intention of the treaties, whatever their form or specific purpose, was to create mutually binding obliga-tions that in theory at least, could not be changed without the consent of both parties (see Wildsmith, 1985, 123-27). Canadian court de-cisions have since placed them somewhere between contracts and promises, which implies, at the very least, moral obligations on the part of the Crown. Amerindians claim international status for them, on the grounds that they were negotiated on a nation-to-nation basis. Such a status has not been formally recognized internationally.

SOME EARLY TREATY TEXTS

The earliest of the British treaty texts that has survived is a 1645 peace accord between the New England Federation and the Narragansetts and Niantics. There were earlier treaties, the first of which was signed in 1620, but none of the texts has been found. The first to include Amerindians in what is now Canada was the Treaty of Portsmouth, New Hampshire, 1713, involving the people of St. John River, mostly Maliseet, but perhaps including some Mi'Kmaq and Abenaki (for the text of the treaty, see Cumming and Mickenberg, eds., 1972, 296-98). Acknowledging themselves "the lawful subjects" of Queen Anne (reign, 1702-14) and promising "hearty Subjection & Obediance unto the Crown of Great Britain," — both of which phrases were typical features of these agreements at the time — the Amerindian signees agreed to desist from hostilities against English settlers. In return, the Amerindians were to enjoy "free liberty for Hunting, Fishing, Fowling, and all other Lawful Liberties & Privileges" and were not to be molested on "their own Grounds." This was the first time such provisions were included in a British/Indian treaty. Later, they became routine. This was the closest that these early peace and friendship treaties came to acknowledging Aboriginal title. Trade, it was stated, would be conducted "in such places & under such management & regulations as shall be stated by her Majesty's Governments."

These terms were repeated in the Treaty of Boston, 1725, which ended active Abenaki resistance to British settlement. That same year saw the British insist on another agreement, also signed in Boston, usually called Treaty No. 239, but also known as Mascarene's Treaty after its principal British negotiator. Its purpose was to get the Mi'Kmaq, Maliseet, and Abenaki to formally recognize that the Treaty of Utrecht (1713) between the British and the French had made the British Crown "the rightful possessor of the Province of Nova Scotia or Acadia according to ancient boundaries." (For the texts of these two treaties, see Cumming and Mickenberg, 1972, 300-04.) The French had included the territories of their Amerindian allies in their cession to Britain without consulting or even informing them, reflecting their non-recognition of Aboriginal title. As far as they were concerned, Acadia was now British. The British, for their part, held that the French occupation and settlement of Acadia by that very fact had extinguished Aboriginal title. The British quickly discovered, however, that the Amerindians held quite a different view. Not only did they not consider that the French had the right to dispose of their territories, particularly without consultation, but they also did not consider that the 1725 treaties in any way implied that the chiefs who signed were acting on behalf of all the Acadian first nations. In other words, they did not accept that one could sign for all unless expressly so authorized by all those affected. In the Amerindian view, at most a chief could sign for was his own immediate band, and then only if its members had been consulted and were in agreement. This, of course, is the doctrine of consent. In the case of the two Boston treaties, this meant arranging ratifications and confirmations so that all the Amerindians of Acadia considered themselves included in their terms. Once this was realized, the British assigned an officer to track down bands that had not signed, a tedious process that proved to be more difficult than expected.

IMPLEMENTING A NEW FOCUS

The Proclamation of 1763, by reserving to the British government the right to acquire Amerindian lands, shifted the principal emphasis of treaties from peace and friendship and acknowledgment of British suzerainty, although they were still present, to negotiating terms by which lands were freed for European settlement. Both Amerindians and Europeans wanted to avoid confrontation, but there the community of aims ended. By the time of the western numbered treaties in the 19th century, the federal government regarded the agreements as the once-and-for-all means of opening up Indian lands for settlement and development, in return for which it granted privileges to be enjoyed at the pleasure of the Crown; for the Amerindians, treaties were a means of safeguarding their rights and getting as favourable a deal as possible. For them, the treaties provided a means for adapting to the demands of a rapidly changing world while still retaining the framework of their own traditions. They sought to provide not only for themselves, but for the generations to come.

The first post-Proclamation treaties were signed in 1764 in southern Ontario. Initially, these were for parcels of land for specific purposes, paid for in cash or goods, and with little thought given to reserving lands for Indians. Sometimes the treaties were not even properly recorded, and often they were imprecise in their terms or in regard to boundaries, giving rise to later disputes. These compacts formed the majority of the 483 treaties listed for Canada in 1912. Since 1975, in Canada, there has been a move to drop the term treaties in favour of agreements, but there has been resistance to this. In contrast, in the United States, there were no treaties signed after 1871.

In one case, the British negotiated a treaty to obtain land for their Iroquois allies, instead of for White settlers. It concerned a tract of 3 million acres (1,214,057 hectares) along either side of the Grand

River in the Niagara Peninsula, and was signed in 1784 by Wabakanine and other Mississauga chiefs with Frederick Haldimand, Governor of Lower Canada from 1778 to 1786. The Iroquois for whom the land was purchased had been dispossessed from their traditional territories in the United States as a consequence of the British losing the American War of Independence (1775-83). Although the original grant has since been much reduced, the Six Nations Reserve is still there, as are other reserves in different locations in Ontario that were set aside for the Iroquois at the same time.

This was a harbinger of large-scale land deals, in which the amounts of land involved grew steadily; in 1850, the Robinson Superior and Robinson Huron Treaties concerned enormous tracts, the largest up to that point. These treaties confirmed the negotiation pattern that had been developing since the Proclamation, and which would soon be followed for the western numbered treaties: terms to be negotiated openly at public meetings, the setting aside of reserves formalized as part of the negotiation procedure instead of on an ad hoc basis; monetary payments to be in the form of annuities to each member of the signing band instead of in a lump sum to the chiefs.

GIFTS BECOME ANNUITIES

Annuities were introduced in the Halifax Treaty of 1752 between the British and the Shubenacadie band of Mi'Kmaq; this treaty has been ruled by the courts as still valid today.[4] In 1752, the annuities substituted for the "gift" distributions by which Amerindians were compensated for their services as allies in the colonial wars. These gifts and the annuities into which they were transformed were usually paid in goods. They had no connection with land surrenders until 1817, when Thomas Douglas, Earl of Selkirk (1771-1820) negotiated for land with Peguis (1774-1864, baptized as William King) at Red River. Selkirk's offer of annual payments in tobacco instead of a one-time cash settlement was accepted. In the official thinking of the day, annuities, whether in cash or in goods, were considered preferable to once-and-for-all cash deals as the payments came out of the proceeds of the sales of the surrendered lands. In effect, Amerindians were indirectly financing their own dispossession. The following year, 1818, the Collingwood Treaty specified the payment of a perpetual annuity of £1,200 in settlement for 1,592,000 acres (644,259 hectares) of land. The 1850 Robinson Treaties contained escalator annuity clauses; this feature, however, was dropped when annuities came to be routinely included in the western numbered treaties. To return to Selkirk's treaty for a moment, it was later repudiated by the Amerindians concerned on the grounds that the signing chiefs had not had the proper authorization from their people.

EARLY "RESERVES" — MISSION VILLAGES

Canada's first "reserve," in Sillery, was established near Quebec City in 1637 on the site of a Montagnais fishing station, on land granted by the French king to the Jesuits "for the benefit of Amerindians." Modeled after the mission villages established by the Jesuits in Brazil, it was the first of several such grants during the French regime. Although title was vested in the missionaries, it was stipulated that the land would be for the use of Amerindians under specified conditions, and that it revert to the French Crown in the event that the Indians abandoned the villages (Henderson, 1980, 2-3; Bartlett, 1984, 2). At Sillery, social problems compounded by overly strict regulations, the rise of alcoholism and Iroquois raids, caused the Amerindians to desert the village by the end of the 17th century; today, it is a prosperous suburb of Quebec City. All of these early mission villages were assigned to the Jesuits. The only exception was Lake of Two Mountains (Oka), granted to the Sulpicians in 1715 "in full property under the title of fief and seigniory," with the proviso that it go to the Sulpicians should the Indians leave. The Sulpicians were the only religious order in Quebec to receive land for their mission on such terms.

The idea of reserving land for exclusive Indian use as a feature of the land-cession treaties was first put forward by the Indians, and was not immediately accepted by the British. The Mississauga of Credit River, for example, had to try several times before they finally won reserved locations (Dickason, 1992, 253). By the time of the two 1850 Robinson Treaties, the idea had taken root, and lists of selected reserve land were appended to each of the treaties. Furthermore, the treaties specified that sales of reserve lands and mineral rights on them were to be conducted by the government for the "sole use and benefit" of the Indians, and only with their consent. This was in line with the fiduciary responsibility that the Crown had assumed when it had reserved to itself the sole right to acquire Amerindian lands in the Proclamation of 1763.

Even so, the official attitude was that reserves were a temporary expedient that would eventually disappear as Amerindians assimilated into mainstream life and adopted the principle of private property. From this perspective, reserves were regarded as providing Amerindians "with a legally recognized tenure of defined lands; in which they have a present right as to the exclusive and absolute usufruct, and a potential right of becoming individual owners in fee after enfranchisement" (*Ontario Reports*, 1885, 231). In social and economic terms, reserves were seen as "the cradle of the Indian civilizing effort — and the means of securing the white man's freedom to exploit the vast riches of a young dominion" (Harper, 1945, 132; Gibbins and Ponting, 1986, 25). Although the treaties allowed Indians to choose the locations of their reserves, officials at first encouraged the selection of small sites near non-Aboriginal settlements. The theory was that such proximity would familiarize Amerindians with Euro-Canadian ways (Federation of Saskatchewan Indians, n.d.), and encourage their adoption, which large reserves in isolated areas would not do (Hodgetts, 1955, 209-10). However, there were other views, such as the one that reserve lands should "be selected in such manner as not to interfere with the possible requirements of future settlement, or of land for railway purposes" (Carter, 1990, 59). In any event, settler pressures for easily available lands discouraged the practice. Not until the 1951 revision of the Indian Act was it made illegal to trespass on reserves and to plunder them for historic artifacts (Shipley, 1968, 327-28).

From the Amerindian perspective, reserves were not granted but were lands that had not been shared with Whites (Federation of Saskatchewan Indians, n.d.). As such they were seen as havens where Amerindians could work out their own accommodations to the changing world. All too often, however, the resources of the reserves were not sufficient for the demands, which, coupled with poorly conceived regulations and administrative practices, meant that many reserve communities sank into poverty and social dysfunction. This was the opposite of what had been originally intended, both by officials and Amerindians.

PRAIRIE WEST AND NORTHWEST

The opening of the prairies for agricultural settlement and of the North for mining during the 19th century made it urgent to deal with Indian land claims in both regions. At the same time Ottawa was also presented with another situation, one that it had not fully examined, and consequently had not expected: the need to help the Indigenous peoples during times of hardship. Both on the prairies and in the North, the situation had arisen because of overexploitation — on the prairies of the buffalo, and in the North of wildlife generally, encouraged by the fur trade. In both areas, this meant that treaty negotiations were not simply concerned with land, but also with providing means to cope with changing ways of life. In the meantime, the First Nations had become increasingly restive as they felt it was unjust "that people who are not owners of the country are allowed to rob them of a living."[5] As the original people, they felt that their rights should have priority; that they kept the peace despite "lawless aggression" on the part of the newcomers speaks volumes for their restraint. "Indian revenge" would have been easy, as Charles Mair (1838-1927), a commissioner for Treaty Eight, wrote (Mair, 1908, 24). Chief Moostoos put it another way during the negotiating sessions at Lesser Slave Lake: "Our country is being broken up. I see the white man coming in, and I want to be friends. I see what he does, but it is best that we be friends" (Mair, 1908, 60). The situation was further complicated by the language and conceptual difficulties that had plagued negotiations from the days of the first encounters. Three centuries of contact had done little to reduce the cultural gap which afflicted both sides. The fact that interpreters for the numbered treaties were usually government representatives was not always helpful for clarifying issues. Anthropologist June Helm had some comments in the case of Treaty Eight (1899):

How could anybody put into the Athapaskan language through a Métis interpreter to monolingual Athapaskan hearers the concept of relinquishing ownership of land, I don't know.... I don't know how they would be able to comprehend the import translated from English into a language which does not have those concepts, and certainly in any sense that Anglo-Saxon jurisprudence would understand.... I don't think they could have.[6]

Another illustration of these difficulties is found in how the word treaty was understood. In the Athapaskan languages, treaty is translated as "money is distributed," or "giving money out": in Chipewyan, *Tsamba Nalye*; in Dogrib, *Samba Nazja*, to give only two examples. In Cree, treaty is translated as *okmaw uso totumā'kewin*, "the chiefs promise" (Fumoleau, 1973, 95, 213; Anderson, 1975, 205, 246).

While it is all too evident that neither side fully understood the conceptual world of the other, it is also clear that the fundamental purpose of treaties — a reciprocal exchange — was generally acknowledged. The problems arose in determining specifics; even those among the Indians who realized that land was at stake only rarely caught the "once-and-for all" aspect of the government's approach. The officials, for their part, had difficulty with the balanced exchange that the Indians expected. Given that "the aim of the Treaty Commission [was] to get the relinquishment of Indian title as cheaply as possible," they placed a much lower value on rights of usage than did the Indians and, consequently, considered the latter's notion of a fair exchange to be extravagant. This disparity in values, even in the terms of the day, was recognized by at least one commissioner, who observed that "the compensation for territorial rights is more fanciful than real."[7]

In any event, Canada's promise to honour the provisions of the 1763 Proclamation led directly to the numbered treaties of the West and Northwest, which began with Treaty One in 1871 and ended with Treaty Eleven in 1921, although adhesions continued to be signed into the 1950s; Treaty Six alone had fifteen. A little more than half of Canada's Amerindians were covered by these arrangements.

The government began the cycle of the western numbered treaties by apparently placing more importance on pomp and ceremony than on the terms of the land surrenders, which were regarded as little more than a formality. The expectation seems to have been to overawe the Amerindians, thus cutting down their demands. The government had been misled. Not only did the Amerindians bargain hard, they remembered exactly what had been verbally promised during the negotiations. They quickly complained when the published texts of Treaties One and Two did not conform to what had been promised. Ottawa's first reaction was to say that the treaties could not be reopened, to which the Amerindians all but accused the government of having obtained the agreements under false pretenses. That made officials much more cautious, as well as more openhanded, in subsequent negotiations. Finally, in 1875, the government revised the offending treaties to bring them into line with Treaty Three, which had been negotiated two years previously along more generous lines.

There were holdouts as the treaty signing progressed. The best-known of these was the half Ojibwa, half Cree Big Bear (Mistahimaskwa, c.1825-1888) who led the largest band of Plains Cree at the time of the negotiations for Treaty Six in 1876. As he saw it, the terms being offered would forfeit his people's autonomy, a view that would be justified by future events. He held out for better terms, but was eventually forced to sign in 1882 in order to get rations for his people who were starving due to the disappearance of the buffalo herds.

INQUIRIES, COMMISSIONS AND REPORTS

Signing, of course, did not automatically ensure that the treaty terms would be kept. The steady tide of complaints, culminating with Treaties Eight and Eleven, finally moved the government to launch a series of investigations to determine what the people had expected, where the problems had occurred, and to recommend ways by which matters could be rectified.

Confusion, misunderstandings and uncertainties abounded on both sides. Where officials considered that a treaty had extinguished Indian title, some bands expressed the view to the Nelson Commission (1956-59) that since their rights to hunt, fish, and trap throughout the Northwest Territories had been guaranteed, that meant that the land belonged to the Indians, as otherwise the guarantees were meaningless. In other words, the Indians did not distinguish between use and ownership, and so did not recognize that they had ceded title to the land while retaining hunting and fishing rights. In their terms, such a division did not make sense. Similarly, an earlier account from the Treaty Eight area in British Columbia noted that the "Beavers [an Indian band] still looked on this country as their own, and upon all whites as usurpers" (Godsell, 1943, 19). Commissioners also found it impossible to make the Indians understand that mineral rights could be separated from actual ownership of land.[8] However, a recommendation to renegotiate the treaty was not acted upon.

Such difficulties have been, and in many cases still are, a constant: different conceptions of the land and its use, of title, of conveying land to others and, as if that were not enough, quite different notions about making contracts. The "take it or leave it" approach favoured by the government had allowed Amerindians very little negotiating room. In Western politics by the end of the 19th century, the doctrine of consent had been long since been modified by the principle of representation — the delegated few speaking for the many. This made it easier for public affairs to be manipulated in favour of special interest groups (Giesey, 1972, 321-32). In other words, public policy was becoming identified with special interests, usually related to business, rather than primarily with people. The First Nations, on the other hand, still operated within the framework of the old values, a position they retain to this day.

This was dramatically illustrated in 1969, when the federal government's White Paper included the termination of the treaties along with its proposal to repeal the Indian Act, thus eliminating special status for Amerindians. The supporting argument held that it was an anomaly for groups within a society to have treaties with their own government. The result of these proposals was to unite the Amerindians as they had never been united before; their opposition was unanimous. They knew what they did not want, which was to be in the same legal category as all other Canadians. The White Paper was withdrawn two years later.

SOME CONCLUDING REMARKS

The social and economic conditions prevailing at the various times and places when the treaties were signed have faded into the past. The agreements, however, are still with us, guiding covenants for more than half of the Aboriginal peoples of Canada. If the immediate concerns that inspired them belong to previous eras, the same cannot be said for their fundamental principles, which still endure. Consequently, they point to the future for both Aboriginal and non-Aboriginal peoples. This is important when interpreting and applying treaty terms: long-range goals that relate to basic principles need to be balanced with short-range and often highly variable considerations. The Aboriginal concept of treaties as living entities that need to be periodically brought into line with altered circumstances has particular pertinence when changes are as rapid and profound as they are today. In some aspects, the ancient perceptions are more relevant than ever.

As we have seen, the principal legal points upon which the First Nations base their position arise from natural law — "inherent right," as the contemporary phrase would have it. Human (statutory) law developed out of natural law as the growing complexities of human societies around the world made it necessary to define the applicability of general principles to specific cases. Ideally, human law translates principles of natural justice into societal justice. That special interests and considerations can — and do — interfere is a reality that is embedded in the very nature of human society, whatever the particular group.

In the days before the arrival of Europeans, the trade networks that crisscrossed the length and breadth of the Americas would not have been possible without corresponding networks of treaties; in other words, diplomacy preceded trade (Rotstein, 1972, 1). Of overriding

concern in these accords were hunting and fishing rights within particular territories, as well as rights of passage through the territories of
others. Elaborate protocols developed around negotiations (as they also
did with trade), the proper observance of which could be as important
as the terms of the agreements themselves. By the time the Europeans
arrived, patterns for treaty negotiations had long since been formalized.

Just as it had been between the various First Nations, so it was
between them and the Europeans — treaties were the principal means
of developing working relationships. These arrangements were fraught
with difficulties from the beginning; even at the time, it was recognized
that cultural differences and widely divergent aims made it extremely
difficult, if it was possible at all, to arrive at agreements that even
approached being mutually satisfactory. The result has been that negotiations, in effect, have never ceased.

Canada has not fully worked out the legal status of the treaties.
While it is clear that they constitute legally enforceable obligations, the
extent to which this can be done in practice has not been clarified. In
spite of the overwhelming evidence of misunderstandings as to just
what was being negotiated, the courts have never been asked to assess
how this affects the status of the treaties as such. This is not a unique
situation, particularly in the realm of international law, where practice
does not often conform to theory, or even to stated goals (Clinebell and
Thomson, 1978, 670). The fact of violations, however, does not mean
that the rights of natural law do not continue to exist.

A good argument could be made that the strength of the First
Nations' position lies with natural law, rather than with the treaties. In
international law, there has been a move toward recognizing the fundamental (or "inherent") rights of Aboriginal peoples. This is a positive
development in a world where the relationship between established
(traditional) principles and adaptation to changing circumstances
needs constant attention. Adaptation is the key to Aboriginal cultural
survival today, just as it was to their physical survival in the days of
the mammoth hunters. Treaties, important as they have been and continue to be in this never-ending process, are still instruments, rather
than ends in themselves.

NOTES

1. Portugal and Spain had signed the Treaty of Tordesillas in 1494, by
   which Spain had agreed to move the papal line dividing Spanish and

Portuguese New World territories 300 leagues to the west. Brazil thus fell within the Portuguese zone.

2. One version attributes the expression to the English King upon concluding a treaty with the Mi'Kmaq of New Brunswick in 1794. The English King is said to have promised to the Indian king: "Henceforth I will provide for you and for the future generations as long as the sun rises and river flows" (cited in Wildsmith, 1985, 154).

3. Champagne, 1994, 472; Thwaites, 1896-1901, vol. 2, 89. The original belt was sent to the Vatican but is now lost. Today it is known through a copy in possession of the Mi'Kmaq Nation.

4. In 1985 the Nova Scotia Supreme Court ruled in *Regina v. Simon* that the 1752 treat was still valid and could only be superseded by federal, not provincial, legislation. See *The Mi'Kmaq Treaty Handbook*, 1987, 13; Marshall, Denny and Marshall, 1989, 71-104.

5. *Report of the Commissioner of the North-West Mounted Police* (1897), 170. The observation was made in connection with the White trappers' custom of using poison bait.

6. Excerpted from Helm's testimony, *Re Paulette et al.*, Supreme Court of Northwest Territories, 1973, 33-34.

7. National Archives of Canada, RG10, Indian Affairs, Black Series, vol. 3848, file 72536-1, letter from McKenna to Sifton, April 17, 1899.

8. National Archives of Canada, 1/1, 11-5, 3-36, *Report of the Commission to Investigate Unfulfilled Provisions of Treaties 8 and 11 as They Apply to the Indians of the Mackenzie District,* 1959 (Nelson Commission).

REFERENCES

Anderson, A., ed. (1975), *Plains Cree Dictionary in the "y" Dialect* (Edmonton: The Author).

Bartlett, R.H. (1984), *Indian Reserves in Quebec* (Saskatoon: University of Saskatchewan Native Law Centre).

Carter, S. (1990), *Lost Harvests: Prairie Indian Reserve Farmers and Government Policy* (Montreal and Kingston: McGill-Queen's University Press).

Champagne, D., ed. (1994), *The Native North American Almanac* (Detroit: Gale Research).

Clinebell, J.H., and J. Thomson (1978), "Sovereignty and Self-Determination: The Rights of Native Americans Under International Law," *Buffalo Law Review*, vol. 27, no. 4, 669-713.

Cumming, P.A., and N.H. Mickenberg, eds. (1972), *Native Rights in Canada* (Toronto: General Publishing).

Dickason, O.P. (1992), *Canada's First Nations: A History of Founding Peoples from Earliest Times*, 1st edn. (Toronto: McClelland & Stewart).

Federation of Saskatchewan Indians (no date), *Indian Treaty Rights* (Saskatoon: Federation of Saskatchewan Indians).

Friesen, J. (1986), "Magnificent Gifts: The Treaties of Canada and the Indians of the Northwest 1869-76," *Transactions of the Royal Society of Canada*, Series 5, vol. 1, 41-51.

Fumoleau, R. (1973), *As Long As This Land Shall Last* (Toronto: McClelland & Stewart).

Gibbins, R., and J.R. Ponting (1986), "Historical Overview and Background," in *Arduous Journey: Canadian Indians and Decolonization*, J.R. Ponting, ed. (Toronto: McClelland & Stewart), 18-56.

Giesey, Ralph E. (1972), "'Quod Omnes Tangit': A Post Scriptum," *Studia Gratiana*, vol. 15, 321-32.

Godsell, Philip H. (1943, 10th edn.), "The Last Covered Wagon Trail," *The Shoulder Strap*, 19.

Harper, A.G. (1945), "Canada's Indian Administration: Basic Concepts and Objectives," *América Indígena*, vol. 2, no. 2, 119-32.

Henderson, W. (1980), *Canada's Indian Reserves: Pre-Confederation* (Ottawa: Department of Indian and Northern Affairs).

Hodgetts, J.E. (1955), *Pioneer Public Service: An Administrative History of the United Canadas, 1841-1867* (Toronto: University of Toronto Press).

Mair, C. (1908), *Through the Mackenzie Basin: Narrative of the Athabaska and Peace River Treaty Expedition of 1899* (Toronto: William Briggs).

Margry, P. (1976-86), *Découvertes et établissements dans l'ouest et dans le sud de l'Amérique septentrionale (1614-1754)*, 6 vols. (Paris: Jouaust), vol. 1.

Marshall, D., Sr., A. Denny, and P.S. Marshall (1989), "The Covenant Chain," in *Drum Beat: Anger and Renewal in Indian Country*, B. Richardson, ed. (Ottawa: Assembly of First Nations), 71-104.

Mi'Kmaq Treaty Handbook (1987), (Sydney and Truro: Native Communications Society of Nova Scotia).

Morris, A. (1862), *The Treaties of Canada with the Indians* (Toronto: Coles Publishing, facs. edn., 1971).

Perrot, N. (c.1644-1717), *Memoire sur les moeurs, coustumes et religion des sauvages de l'Amérique septentrionale*, J. Tailhan, ed. (Montréal: Editions Elysées, 1973).

Ross, R. (1996), *Returning to the Teachings: Exploring Aboriginal Justice* (Toronto: Penguin).

Rotstein, A. (1972), "Trade and Politics: An Institutional Approach," *Western Canadian Journal of Anthropology*, vol. 3, no. 1, 1-28.

Royal Commission on Aboriginal Peoples (1996), *Report of the Royal Commission on Aboriginal Peoples*, 5 vols. (Ottawa: Minister of Supply and Services Canada).

Scott, J.B. (1934), The Spanish Conception of International Law and of Sanctions (Washington: Carnegie Endowment for International Peace).

Shipley, N. (1968), "Twilight of the Treaties," *Queen's Quarterly*, vol. 70, no. 3, 312-29.

Thwaites, R.G., ed. (1896-1901), *Jesuit Relations and Allied Documents*, 73 vols. (Cleveland: Burrows Bros.), vols. 2, 55.

Warren, W. (1984), *History of the Ojibway People* (St. Paul: Minnesota Historical Society).

Wildsmith, B. (1985), "Pre-Confederation Treaties," in *Aboriginal People and the Law: Indian, Métis and Inuit Rights in Canada*, B.W. Morse, ed. (Ottawa: Carleton University Press), 122-271.

7

LISTENING AND HEEDING: CHALLENGES OF RESTRUCTURING THE RELATIONSHIP BETWEEN ABORIGINAL PEOPLES AND CANADA

Jackie Wolfe-Keddie

RESTRUCTURING AND ABORIGINAL PEOPLES

PERKSON (1993) USES THE TERM "PLASTIC WORDS" to describe the way in which particular words or phrases take on newly nuanced meanings when they are appropriated by "expert" groups (academics, "spin-doctors," politicians, lobbyists, corporate interests, public relations people and others). Like Salvador Dali's "plastic" clocks, the words first shock, excite, alarm, and challenge, but repeated by imitators and popularizers, they become "buzz words," and their meaning blurs.

Restructuring is one such "plastic word." "Global restructuring," "corporate restructuring," "government restructuring," and many other types of restructuring are widely understood to be linked to the globalization of the world's economy accompanied by massive structural change, and the planned or incremental responses by governments and organizations across the globe to capture some of the positive effects of these changes and reduce their negative impacts. The central government of New Zealand has restructured its social welfare state-led economy, aspects of which are explored in the chapters in this volume by Joseph and Knight and especially by Moran. The provincial government of Ontario is restructuring the municipal government and administration of the province's largest metropolis, Toronto. The City of Waterloo, Ontario, has restructured in the image of a private corporation and has adopted the self-describing slogan, Waterloo Inc.

On the other hand, Indigenous peoples, whose lands were appropriated and whose cultures, economies and political lives changed irreversibly by the colonization processes (Miller, 1989; Berger, 1991), continue to confront the multiple and massive economic and political impacts of past global restructuring while dealing at the same time with its contemporary forms. Maori in New Zealand are striving to use the Waitangi Tribunal (established in 1975) to implement terms of the 1840 Treaty of Waitangi (Stokes, 1992). Australian Aborigines have been attempting, with limited success, to engage governments and the citizens of Australia in enacting a treaty that gives a moral and legal basis for reconciliation and for improved relationships.

Aboriginal peoples in Canada are no exception. They, like the Maori and Australian Aborigines, are calling for change. And like the Maori and Australian Aborigines, their emphasis is on the "restructuring of the relationship" between Indigenous peoples and the state — between Aboriginal peoples and non-Aboriginal peoples of Canada (Royal Commission on Aboriginal Peoples [RCAP], vol. 2, 1996). This paper explores what restructuring means in this context, and why it is so elusive.

"TELL US WHAT YOU WANT": A BRIEF REVIEW OF THE CANADIAN RECORD OF LISTENING AND HEEDING

The inability or unwillingness of Canadian politicians and the Canadian public to maintain a concern for Aboriginal peoples and Aboriginal issues long enough to come to understand them and to commit to substantive structural changes in relationships (relationships that continue to be destructive of Aboriginal society and are a recurring embarrassment for Canadian society) is not new. It is a continuing reality experienced by generations of Aboriginal peoples in Canada as they seek to gain sustained attention from Canadians and Canadian politicians — and fail repeatedly.

To cite some recent examples: in 1969 the Liberal federal government's White Paper proposed a policy for a "just society" for Indians which would end any recognition of special status for Indians and would dismantle the apparatus of the Department of Indian Affairs. The response from the First Nations was swift, unequivocal and unanimously negative. Harold Cardinal, then President of the Indian Association of Alberta countered with *The Unjust Society: The Tragedy of Canada's Indians* (Cardinal, 1969), a treatise quickly dubbed the "Red Paper."

During the heated and often bitter debates in the early 1980s prior to the patriation of the Canadian constitution, an exasperated Prime Minister Trudeau was captured on national television demanding of Aboriginal elders and other leaders, "just tell us what you want!" What Aboriginal leaders wanted was full constitutional recognition and protection of Aboriginal rights. In July 1981 they found that reference to Aboriginal rights had been dropped. After prolonged and intense negotiation by Aboriginal leaders, they succeeded in getting some reference to Aboriginal rights in the constitution. Section 35(1) of the Constitution Act, 1982, recognizes "existing Aboriginal and treaty rights." There are, however, fundamental differences between Aboriginal peoples and the federal and provincial governments as to the spirit and intent of "existing Aboriginal rights," and "treaty rights" (Imai, *et al.*, 1993). Aboriginal people were promised a special constitutional conference with First Ministers (federal and provincial) to discuss "matters that directly affect the Aboriginal peoples of Canada, including identification and definition of the rights of Aboriginal peoples referred to but not defined in the Constitution of Canada." In all, four constitutional conferences were held (in 1983, 1984, 1985 and 1987) without agreement being reached on the nature of those rights or on any major issue, including the right of Aboriginal peoples to self-government.

In 1991, more than twenty years after the White Paper and the Red Paper, the then Conservative federal government struck a Royal Commission to review the impact of nearly four hundred years of contact with settlers on the Indigenous peoples of the "winter half" of the continent, and to make recommendations to the federal government. The Commission was, in large part, the government's response to the summer-long confrontation between Mohawk and Quebec and Canadian civil and military authorities over proposed development authorized by the municipality of Oka on land claimed by the Mohawk of Kanasatake; increasingly frequent acts of civil disobedience (road blockades) by some Aboriginal groups; and growing criticism on the part of Aboriginal peoples across Canada about the way in which the issues were being handled by all levels of government.

The mandate conferred on the Commission was, arguably, the broadest in the history of Canadian royal commissions. The Commission was asked to look at virtually every aspect of the lives of the First Nations and Inuit and Métis peoples of Canada — their history, health and education; their aspirations for self-government and their relationships with Canadian governments; their land claims, treaties, economies and cultures; their living conditions in cities as well as on reserves, and in the North; their experiences with the justice system; the state of their languages; their spiritual well-being; and, more generally, their situation in Canada relative to that of non-Aboriginal Canadians (RCAP, vol. 5, appendix C, 1996, 296).

In carrying out the monumental task of reviewing the past and present relationship between Aboriginal peoples (estimated as being between 1 million and 1.5 million people) and Canada, and of making recommendations that would positively restructure that relationship, the seven commissioners and their staff visited hundreds of communities and received testimony at public hearings; solicited briefs and submissions from individuals and organizations; organized national round tables on Aboriginal issues; and carried out a major program of research studies and publication. The total cost of the Commission and its consultations, research and publications was just over $51 million.

ABORIGINAL PEOPLE TELL THEIR STORY ONCE AGAIN:
FINDINGS OF THE 1991-1996 ROYAL COMMISSION
ON ABORIGINAL PEOPLES

The Royal Commission presented its findings to the federal government (by then Liberal) and the Canadian public in October 1996 in a comprehensive five-volume final report, accompanied by a 103-page briefing guide to the principle findings and recommendations of the final report (RCAP, 5 vols., 1996), *People to People: Nation to Nation* (RCAP, 1996a), which highlights the commission's findings and conclusions, and a CD-ROM that includes not only the final report but also the interim reports and all the major research documents.

The Commission found, as had many previous analyses (Hawthorne, 1967; Penner 1983), that the government of Canada has pursued contradictory policies of assimilation, protection, separation and neglect (Table 5) which have been destructive of Aboriginal societies, governments and economies. Implementation of the policies has perpetrated multi-layered injustices on Aboriginal peoples across Canada (Table 6).

The first volume, *Looking Forward: Looking Back* (RCAP, vol. 1, 1996), describes the rhythms and changes in Aboriginal life prior to contact with European settlers, and the changing nature of the relationship between Aboriginal and non-Aboriginal people over the last five hundred years, making use of vignettes illustrating the experience of particular Aboriginal peoples. The second volume, *Restructuring the Relationship*, explores the structural factors that define the political and

TABLE 5

INSTRUMENTS OF ASSIMILATION, PROTECTION, SEPARATION, AND NEGLECT

- the Indian Act;
- break-up of historic Aboriginal nations and creation of band and community governments;
- state legislation dictating who is recognized as Indian;
- forced attendance of generations of Aboriginal children at residential schools;
- relocation of Aboriginal people into centralized settlements and relocation of score of Aboriginal communities;
- adoption of Aboriginal children into non-Aboriginal homes;
- loss of two-thirds of land set aside in treaties as Aboriginal land;
- exclusion of Aboriginal input and Aboriginal culture from process relating to education, justice, health and family services;
- substitution of welfare for an effective economic base.

TABLE 6

A SOCIAL CRISIS

- poverty: earned income per employed Aboriginal individual $14,561, compared with $24,001 for all Canadians in 1991;
- dependency: 46 percent of people resident on reserves live on welfare;
- low educational attainment: 42 percent of Aboriginal children complete grade 12 compared with 61 percent of the broader population;
- low labour force participation: Aboriginal labour force participation is 57 percent compared with 68 percent for all Canadians;
- high unemployment: rates of unemployment of those *in* the labour force rose from 15.4 percent in 1981 to 24.6 percent in 1991 (despite some advances in educational attainment over the period);
- poor health: for example, incidence of TB is 17 times higher and diabetes three times higher than for the general population;
- excessive expenditures: governments spend 57 percent more on Aboriginal peoples than on the same number of other Canadians, largely for remedial measures and social assistance (though part of this is due to higher costs of servicing remote communities).

Source: Adapted from *Guide to the Principal Findings and Recommendations of the Final Report of the Royal Commission on Aboriginal Peoples* (1996b), 4.

economic power exercised by Canadian governments, and identifies what it regards as "the four basic pillars of the new relationship: treaties, governance, lands and resources, and economic development" (RCAP, vol. 2, 2). The two-part volume includes a detailed examination of Aboriginal traditions of governance and possible models of self-government. *Gathering Strength* (RCAP, vol. 3, 1996) addresses in detail the measures needed to renew and rebuild Aboriginal peoples, communities and nations. *Perspectives and Realities* (RCAP, vol. 4, 1996) explores the circumstances of Aboriginal women, elders, youth, the Métis, and the particular challenges facing those who live in the far North and those who live in urban environments, and gives voice to their concerns. Finally, *Renewal: A Twenty-Year Commitment* (RCAP, vol. 5, 1996) integrates the findings and analysis into a multifaceted, multi-year strategy to reform the foundations of the relationship, and to use this as the basis from which to restructure the economic and political institutions supporting Aboriginal culture and societies.

THE ROYAL COMMISSION ON ABORIGINAL PEOPLES RECOMMENDS RESTRUCTURING THE RELATIONSHIP BETWEEN ABORIGINAL AND NON-ABORIGINAL SOCIETIES IN CANADA

In the words of the Commissioners:

We have made recommendations affecting virtually every aspect of Aboriginal peoples' lives. We have sought to grapple with entrenched economic and social problems in Aboriginal communities while also seeking to transform the relationship between Aboriginal nations and Canadian governments ... the problems are rendered more challenging by their interdependence. The scale and complexity of the task is daunting (RCAP, vol. 5, 1996, 1).

The Commission grounds its recommendations in principles which are themselves the foundation stones of properly functioning Aboriginal society. The first recommendation, that "the federal, provincial and territorial governments, on behalf of the people of Canada, and national Aboriginal organizations, on behalf of Aboriginal peoples of Canada, commit themselves to building a renewed relationship based on the principles of mutual recognition, mutual respect, sharing and mutual responsibility" underpins all those that follow. In its concern for establishing a relationship between Aboriginal and non-Aboriginal peoples based on mutuality, respect and shared responsibility, and in its advocacy for restructuring the institutions intended to serve Aboriginal interests, it shares much with the proposals for restructuring enunciated by Maori, Australian Aborigines, and other Indigenous peoples around the globe.

The key components for the rebalancing of the political relationship (as adapted from RCAP, 1996b, 7) include:

- restoration of the rights to self-government;
- restoration of control of an adequate land base;
- recognition that Aboriginal culture and values differ in many ways from the organizing principles of non-Aboriginal society;
- restructuring of institutions of governance, education, health, justice and economic development according to these distinctive principles;
- according Aboriginal communities who come together as nations with government jurisdiction as one of three recognized orders of government in Canada;
- supporting Aboriginal nation governments with new fiscal arrangements and recognizing their taxation authority;
- engaging with Aboriginal nations in the interpretation or renewal of existing treaties or the negotiation of new treaties that determine the jurisdiction of Aboriginal governments and their land and resource base;
- reallocating lands and resources to provide an adequate economic base to promote self-reliance of individuals and the financing of Aboriginal governments.

These are the same matters that Aboriginal peoples have struggled to keep on the national agenda for decades, if not centuries. They are matters on which some progress has been achieved, through the determination of Aboriginal peoples and their leaders to use all means necessary, including the courts, to get the agenda addressed.

The Royal Commission spells out in some detail the legislation necessary to secure a restructured and mutually respectful relationship (Table 7). Achievement of this agenda would give Aboriginal people decision making authority over those matters which affect them most directly — their governments and the land and resources they control — and would provide for full expression of Aboriginal cultural differences.

The more than four hundred detailed recommendations cover virtually all aspects of Aboriginal life. Many are modest. Many are statements of common sense or appropriate practice in relationships. Several are already being implemented in some parts of Canada, though not necessarily as national policy (for example 3.5.8, "All schools serving Aboriginal children adopt policies that welcome the involvement of Aboriginal parents, elders and families in the life of the school ...").

TABLE 7

ACTS OF PARLIAMENT RECOMMENDED BY THE ROYAL
COMMISSION TO IMPLEMENT THE RESTRUCTURING
OF THE RELATIONSHIP

- Preparation of a new Royal Proclamation (replacing the Royal Proclamation of 1763) acknowledging the mistakes of the past and committing governments to a new relationship and preparation of companion legislation including:
- Aboriginal Nation Recognition and Government Act to officially recognize legitimate Aboriginal nations and provides for new fiscal arrangements to finance their activities;
- Aboriginal Treaties Implementation Act to establish principles and processes by which recognized nations could renew their existing treaties or create new ones. The Act would establish regional Treaty Commissions to facilitate and support treaty negotiations;
- Aboriginal Lands and Treaties Tribunal Act to decide on specific claims, ensure that treaty negotiations are conducted and financed fairly, and protect the interests of affected parties;
- Aboriginal Parliament Act to represent Aboriginal peoples within federal governing institutions and advise Parliament on matters affecting Aboriginal people. A Constitutional Amendment would eventually create a House of First Peoples, to join the House of Commons and the Senate as constituting the Parliament of Canada;
- Aboriginal Relations Department and Indian and Inuit Services Department Act to replace the Department of Indian and Northern Affairs, and, in the first case, to implement the new relationship with Aboriginal peoples, and in the second, to administer services for communities that have not yet opted for self-government.

Source: Adapted from *Guide to the Principal Findings and Recommendations of the Final Report of the Royal Commission on Aboriginal Peoples* (1996b), 9.

To be properly implemented, many, such as 2.3.18 which calls for financing mechanisms for Aboriginal governments to be based "not only on revenue raising capacity but also on differences in the expenditure needs of the Aboriginal governments," require major infusions of "new" money. Indeed, the Commission argues that the significant increases in funding over the next 15 years, which it recommends, are a sound investment in the future of Aboriginal peoples in Canada, and that the cost to the state of *not* making these investments will be much higher.

Some, such as the proposal to establish a process "for identifying Aboriginal groups entitled to exercise the right of self-determination as nations" and to vest the right of self-government in those nations (Table 7), or 2.3.51, "the federal government, following extensive consultations with Aboriginal peoples, establish an Aboriginal parliament," are highly controversial both within and beyond the Aboriginal domain (Rowse, 1992).

Finally, the Commission recommends (5.1.1.) that First Ministers, territorial leaders and leaders of the national Aboriginal organizations meet within six months of the release of the report to review the principal recommendations, to begin consultations on drafting and enactment of a Royal Proclamation redefining the nature of the relationships between Aboriginal nations and the Canadian government, and to establish a forum to create a Canada-wide Framework Agreement.

In its recommendations, the Commission has addressed simultaneously the two dominant Aboriginal agendas: (1) the grand agenda, which insists that the future for Aboriginal people lies in achieving structural change and passage of laws that secure their governments, their lands and their resources against policy shifts by successive federal, provincial and territorial governments, and that this agenda is not only worth waiting for, it is the essential agenda for all Aboriginal people; and (2) the immediate, localized and incremental agendas of specific peoples who desire to implement now those changes that will enable them to deal better with the present and which may, cumulatively, result in some structural change over the long-term.

We will now examine the responses to the Royal Commission and its recommendations, identify the many barriers obstructing the achievement of the agenda and, finally, discuss some of the steps that are underway and their implications.

RESPONSES TO RECOMMENDATIONS
FROM THE ROYAL COMMISSION ON ABORIGINAL PEOPLES

Much of the public and political response as reported by the print media, radio and television was swift, unequivocal and destructive. Condemnations included the following: the 4000-page report was unreadable and indigestible; the recommendations were too numerous, too sweeping, or too trivial. Major structural changes were labelled revolutionary, or politically naive. Specific recommendations, particularly those which called for new or expanded Aboriginal administrative, decision making, and service delivery agencies were lambasted as being irresponsible and contradictory to the prevailing trend for downsizing and reduction in the machinery of government. The proposals for significant increases in financial support for Aboriginal communities, organizations and programs, were dismissed as unrealistic, particularly in a period of national fiscal restraint.

Despite several consultations on the recommendations of the Report with assemblies of First Nations, well-attended public conferences immediately following the release of the report, and appeals to the government from Aboriginal leaders such as Ovide Mercredi, immediate past Grand Chief, Assembly of First Nations, and Phil Fontaine, former Grand Chief of the Assembly of Manitoba Chiefs and now Grand Chief of the Assembly of First Nations, to follow the Report's recommendation and hold formal consultations on the Report's recommendations, the Royal Commission on Aboriginal Peoples has received only sporadic public attention and little political action. Aboriginal issues played virtually no part in the federal election held eight months after the release of the Report. Canadian public policy continued to be made for Aboriginal peoples with little or no direct reference to the work of the Commission.

Finally, in late 1997, the federal government unveiled *Gathering Strength — Canada's Aboriginal Action Plan.* The government's response included a specific apology to the victims of sexual and physical abuse at residential schools, and $450 million to support community-based healing programs as a means of dealing with the legacy of abuse. It set out four broad objectives: renewing partnerships; strengthening Aboriginal governance; developing a new fiscal relationship; and supporting strong communities, people and economies. In its response, the government has used the Commission's terminology of "renewed relationship," emphasized the rhetoric of "partnership," and espoused negotiation rather than legislation or litigation as the preferred approach to deal with issues. And quietly, with no public fanfare, the government has endorsed the Aboriginal right to self-government, albeit a very limited right, which it had so long resisted, stating: "these government-to-government relationships will be consistent with the treaties, the recognition of the inherent right of self-government, Aboriginal title, and Aboriginal and treaty rights under section 35 of the Constitution Act, 1982" (Minister of Indian Affairs and Northern Development, 1998).

The Royal Commission on Aboriginal Peoples is only the most recent, most costly, most thorough and comprehensive review of the relationships between Aboriginal peoples and the people and governments of Canada. Aboriginal peoples have protested directly to the governments and the courts of Canada for several centuries about the loss of their land and resources, the suppression of their governments, languages, and cultural practices, and the destruction of their life-ways and societies. Aboriginal leaders repeatedly tell the government and the people of Canada "what they want." Successive governments unveil responses, policies and plans. Regardless, the massive intrusion of Canadian governments and, increasingly, corporate interests, into the lives of Aboriginal peoples continues.

RESTRUCTURING IN THE CONTEXT OF DOMINATION, ADAPTATION, AND RESISTANCE

A wide array of explanations has been offered for this impasse. Political and social critics have argued that a major problem is the inability of Aboriginal peoples and their leaders to speak with one voice concerning the causes for the problematic positioning of Aboriginal peoples within the Canadian state, and their inability to offer a few straightforward, understandable and politically acceptable remedies. There is substance to this claim. The recommendations of the Royal Commission were numerous and complex. Several Aboriginal peoples and organizations did not participate in the hearings of the Commission. Others distanced themselves from the Commission Report and have been highly critical of all or part of the recommendations proposed by RCAP. But there are many sound reasons why analysis and solutions are complex, and why Aboriginal peoples across Canada do not, and cannot speak with one voice on issues.

An alternative explanation invokes the preoccupation of non-Aboriginal society with its own issues, agendas and crises, not the least of which is the national obsession with the future of Canada with or without Quebec, which repeatedly displaces any brief public attention that Aboriginal matters may have gained. A related explanation invokes the notion that the Aboriginal "problem" is so out of keeping with the concerns and interests of the dominant society that it does not hold public attention. Indeed, the Canadian public is so tuned out and turned off Aboriginal issues that more than half the people questioned in a 1997 survey believed that Aboriginal peoples in Canada were better or as well off as other Canadians, or had no opinion on the matter. Aboriginal leaders and some analysts hint at but seldom express the idea that deeply rooted racism plays a part in public ignorance and political lack of will.

Scholarly inquiry into Aboriginal/non-Aboriginal relations has been dominated by two modes of analysis (Satzewich and Wotherspoon, 1993). One applies variants on the colonialism and dependency model, in this case internal colonialism and what Beckett (1988) calls welfare colonialism, to understand the establishment of unequal and exploitative relationships and the exercise of external social, political and economic controls over the Indigenous peoples (Boldt, 1981; Coates and Powell, 1989; Frideres, 1998; Watkins, 1972). The other explores the processes of acculturation or assimilation and the consequences of these, with particular emphasis on the negative consequences for Aboriginal peoples. While offering useful insights into causes and effects, neither mode of analysis has produced much in the way of constructive solutions.

More recently, analysts have applied variants of a political economy approach: an approach that examines the way in which changing material and political circumstances shape and are shaped by Aboriginal life experiences, namely, the incorporation of Aboriginal territories into a majority settler state under liberal-democratic government and under capitalism (Satzewich and Wotherspoon, 1993; Andersen, 1995). This approach focuses more directly than the previous two on themes of domination and subordination, adaptation and resistance, as Aboriginal peoples struggle for survival in a multicultural late capitalist state, itself restructuring politically, economically and socially in response to internal and global forces. A theme of such analysis is the rebalancing of unequal relationships, and its corollary, the affirmation of Aboriginal cultures and Aboriginal rights, particularly the collective right to make decisions on those matters directly affecting Aboriginal peoples.

Many Aboriginal people place emphasis on the deep destruction of the spirit that they and their communities have experienced, and regard empowerment less as a political activity and more as a deep spiritual and healing process. Others speak of personal and mutual responsibilities, mutual respect and trust as ways of rebuilding both Aboriginal society and relationships with the wider society of Canada. Many Aboriginal leaders spend long hours at negotiating tables with federal and provincial bureaucrats and lawyers in pursuit of satisfactory agreements on treaties and land rights, greater self-government, and myriad interconnected issues. Others pursue similar agendas through the mechanisms of the courts, where, from time to time judgements like *Sparrow,* 1990, and *Delgamuukw* 1997, set precedents in support of Aboriginal rights. When individuals and communities find no redress in negotiation or in the courts, they resort to forms of civil disobedience and direct protest, for example, blockading roads.

More subtle explanations cite fundamental differences between the principles and practices of Aboriginal societies and the principles and

practices of Canadian settler society, which inhibit effective communication and stand in the way of achieving agreements that are mutually
satisfactory. These, then, are some of the understandings and misunderstandings of restructuring in the Aboriginal domain (Rowse, 1992).

BARRIERS TO LISTENING, HEEDING, AND SUPPORTING A RESTRUCTURED RELATIONSHIP

In this exploration of the challenges faced by First Nations as they seek
to restructure the relationship between themselves and non-Aboriginal
Canada, I will pursue several themes which act as barriers to listening,
heeding, and mutual restructuring of relationships: demographics;
agendas; many peoples-many voices; the implications for decision making; and Aboriginal understanding of relationships. Under the rubric of
demographics and other agendas, I explore the many ways in which, in
Canada, Aboriginal societies and non-Aboriginal society are out of step
to such a degree that Aboriginal priorities and modus operandi are very
different from those of their "fellow Canadians" or, when they are
similar, are not understood to be so. Next, I challenge as unrealistic the
expectation that there can be a set of simple solutions to what are highly complex issues, and argue that there are good reasons why Aboriginal
people speak with many voices, not one voice, and that these voices are
to be expected, and should be respected and heeded. Aboriginal people
have resisted, adapted to, and challenged the prevailing relationships in
different ways. Through both of these I contemplate the ways in which
Aboriginal peoples and non-Aboriginal society reach decisions, and the
importance placed by Aboriginal society on sound and proper relationships. Then I focus discussion on the Aboriginal emphasis on restructuring of relationships. Particular difficulties arise when Aboriginal
societies, whose ways of relating and coming to decisions are in large
part still based on the principles and practices of social compact, "meet"
with Canadian society, which bases its formal negotiations and agreements on civil contract, and then attempt to reach a mutually satisfactory set of decisions and get action on them.

Demographics

The demographic and economic profile of the Aboriginal population is
dramatically different from the non-Aboriginal population of Canada
(Table 8). It is growing faster. It is much more youthful. It is much
poorer. It is much less urban.

According to Statistics Canada, the number of people in Canada of Aboriginal ancestry is expected to increase from somewhat over 1.1 million in 1991 to between 1.5 and 1.7 million in 2019, still a relatively small minority in a population of over 27 million. In 1991, 36 percent of the Aboriginal population was under the age of 15, compared with 20.6 percent for Canada as a whole. In 1991, just under three percent of the Aboriginal population was 65 or over, whereas 11.6 percent of Canada's population was over 65. Almost half of all Aboriginal people who earn any income at all, earn less than $10,000 per year, compared with 27 percent for all Canadians. Similarly 73.4 percent of Aboriginal people have incomes of less than $20,000 compared with 52.1 percent for all Canadians. While over half the number of people of Aboriginal ancestry live at any one time in urban areas, the proportion of people of Aboriginal origin who live in small and/or isolated communities is much higher than the national average.

The implications for both Aboriginal and non-Aboriginal Canadians of these differences are profound. A significant proportion of Canada's population are members of a large and relatively affluent class of aging babyboomers, their children, and their elderly parents. Not surprisingly, income and job security, quality health care, quality education, the ups and downs of the stock and bond markets, mortgage rates, home ownership, protection against crimes against person and property, leisure activities, retirement planning, pension protection, and care and accommodation for the elderly are some of their many concerns; in summary, protection of economic advantage. These are also the people who participate most actively and vociferously in political debate. Political parties seeking re-election cannot afford to ignore their concerns.

TABLE 8

A DEMOGRAPHIC CRISIS

- The Aboriginal population is growing at twice the rate of the Canadian population;
- 56 percent of the Aboriginal population is below the age of 25, with two thirds of these below 15 years of age;
- to reach the 9-10 percent rate of unemployment of the Canadian population today (itself considered unacceptable) 300,000 new jobs will have to be created and held by Aboriginal people in the next 20 years.

Source: Adapted from *Guide to the Principal Findings and Recommendations of the Final Report of the Royal Commission on Aboriginal Peoples* (1996b), 6.

The priorities of the majority of Aboriginal peoples, families and communities have a qualitatively different focus: how to raise levels of individual and household income above poverty levels; how to provide meaningful employment in remote locations and in the poorest of urban neighbourhoods, especially for undereducated youth; how to deal with the apathy, rage and violence, again particularly of youth; how to reduce the chronic overcrowding in reserve housing; how to provide the basic necessities of running water and waste water disposal for all households; how to improve the levels of health and reduce alcohol and drug abuse; how to improve the life expectancy of infants and cope with the consequences of fetal alcohol syndrome; how to curb physical and sexual abuse; how to end youth and young adult suicide; in summary, healing and cultural survival, as well as economic improvements (Table 9).

Clearly there are some commonalities between these two sets of issues: for example, the education of youth, under and unemployment, especially, but not exclusively, of youth, abuse against children and women, and crimes of violence against persons and property are over-lapping concerns. However, in many small isolated Aboriginal communities, where over half of the population is under the age of 16, the interrelated issues are, almost literally, overwhelming, and seemingly intractable.

TABLE 9

REBUILDING OF CAPACITY IN INDIVIDUALS AND COMMUNITIES

- Integrating health and social services in Aboriginal controlled delivery institutions that see healing as the treatment of the whole person in his or her environment;
- training 10,000 Aboriginal health professionals;
- instituting broad programs for maternal care and early childhood education;
- accelerating the development of Aboriginal education systems through curriculum development, training of large numbers of Aboriginal teachers and administrators, and encouraging Aboriginal control of education policy and schools on Aboriginal territory;
- accelerating economic development with the design and delivery of business programs in the hands of Aboriginal institutions and the creation of a National Aboriginal Development Bank;
- Developing intensive measures with all major private and public sector employers in regions of significant Aboriginal population to provide on-the-job training;
- restructuring social welfare to permit able-bodied individuals to work or be trained, thereby strengthening the economic and social infrastructure of communities;
- expanding Aboriginal justice services and promoting the evolution of distinctive Aboriginal justice systems.

Source: Compiled by the author from *Guide to the Principal Findings and Recommendations of the Final Report of the Royal Commission on Aboriginal Peoples* (1996b).

Other Agendas

Across much of Canada, local and provincial governments are trying out new ways to cover the cost of maintaining and expanding physical infrastructure (roads, water and sewage, and other public utilities). Aboriginal communities that are physically isolated, and/or hidden behind the invisible barrier of the reserve, experienced decades of neglect. The costs of catch-up to provide even basic physical infrastructure of running water, waste water disposal and sound if simple housing, are high. Most non-Aboriginal Canadians have little understanding of the reasons why Aboriginal communities are poorly serviced, and are presumed by federal and provincial politicians (probably correctly) to be unwilling to countenance increased diversion of public funding to such causes. Deficit and debt reduction followed by tax reduction are key and popular features of national and provincial governments' agendas, not tax increases to fund new or expanded programs for Aboriginal communities.

In the last 20 years, Aboriginal issues have, with some regularity, hit the national headlines and held the national interest for a few months, only to be displaced by a national crisis arising from the struggle of Quebec separatists to assert their separate identity and sovereignty. This restructuring of the political map of Canada, not the restructuring proposed by Aboriginal people has, of course, the greatest potential to change the face of Canada and the future for Canadians. Scenarios contemplating the effects of separation of all or parts of Quebec from the rest of Canada are, with the obvious exception of those proposed by the Parti Québécois, generally pessimistic about the effects of separation on the economy and society of both Canada and Quebec. Hence, the national obsession with "the Quebec issue" (Knight, 1998). With a few exceptions, the most notable being within the Six Nations, Aboriginal leaders, peoples, nations, communities and organizations accept that their future lies within Canada, not outside of it. They do not seek to sever the relationship with Canada and their fellow Canadians. They seek to restructure and then rebuild it.

Aboriginal leaders are, consequently, faced with the problem of trying to gain attention for matters which, in so many different ways, are out of step with national priorities. And they do so, not as one minority among many within the Canadian body politic, but as many sub-minorities, each with its own needs and its own perspectives on what is needed to make significant change, on what works and what does not.

Many Peoples: Many Voices

When they refer to Aboriginal peoples collectively as natives, Indians, Aboriginals, or special interests or stakeholders, Canadian politicians, bureaucrats, researchers, the media, and citizens oversimplify the political, cultural and linguistic richness of Aboriginal peoples in Canada, and diminish their status as cultural and political nations.

Of course, there never was a single Aboriginal culture. Rather, there were many peoples with their own languages, social organizations, cultural practices, forms of government, and life-ways adapted to the geographical conditions of different parts of the country: Dene, Mi'Kmaq, Nishga'a, Cree, Innu, to name but a few. Moreover, their cultures were not static. New materials, food stuffs and cultural practices spread from one group to another, and were adapted and transformed in the process of diffusion (Trigger, 1985, 50-163). Each people had methods of exercising social regulation and control and internal decision making, and had developed conventions for dealing with other peoples; that is, they had their own forms of government, which varied from one people to another, and changed in response to new opportunities and new threats (Trigger, 1985). Agreements between peoples, as Dickason points out in this volume, were not introduced to the Americas by the Europeans. Alliances and methods of "treating" with neighbours had long been institutionalized, and carried with them mutual understanding of what trust and honour meant in such relationships, together with mutual acceptance of the consequences should any party dishonour an agreement.

The processes of contact with European settlers, and the methods used by Canadian political, administrative and ecclesiastical authorities to carry out deliberate policies of assimilation, on the one hand, and separation between Aboriginal peoples and other residents on the other, brought about massive transformations within Aboriginal societies in Canada. In one or two generations, many individuals lost their ability to speak the language of their people, and lost much of their cultural heritage, their land base and their economy. This process started earlier (at the end of the 16th century and beginning of the 17th century) and has lasted longer in eastern and southern Canada than elsewhere. In more remote and northern regions, the most dramatic

impacts of coerced movement of Aboriginal people into small centralized settlements did not take place until well into the 20th century.
The mechanisms of cultural transformation, the church, formal schooling, and a cash economy have, in the latter part of the 20th century,
been augmented by the financial citizen entitlements provided to individuals and families through the social safety-net of the welfare state
in the form of family support payments, income supplements and
unemployment benefits, and by the penetration of television into even
the most remote community.

The process of colonization has also divided Aboriginal peoples by
imposing distinctions between those who Canadian law (as enunciated
in the Indian Act) recognizes as Indian (members of First Nations), and
those of Indian heritage who the law excludes (Non-Status Indians,
and Métis). And, of course, the Indian Act sets Aboriginal people apart
from all other citizens of Canada by making Status Indians subject
to the Indian Act, which applies to virtually all aspects of their lives
(government, wills and inheritances, possession of land on reserves),
but is not applicable to any other citizen.

The treaties, discussed in detail by Dickason in this volume,
similarly set apart those Aboriginal peoples who were signatories to
the historic Treaties of Peace and Friendship (in what became New
Brunswick and Nova Scotia) and the named and numbered treaties (for
example, the Robinson-Huron 1850, Robinson-Superior 1850,
Manitoulin Island Treaty 1862, Williams Treaties 1923, and Treaties
1-11, 1871-1921) from those Aboriginal peoples who did not, and
from all other citizens of Canada not subject to formal treaties.

The named and numbered treaties formalize the physical separation of Treaty Indians through the establishment, under the terms of
the treaties, of small parcels of land set aside and reserved to Indians, in
exchange for surrender of title to all lands otherwise occupied by those
Indians, and in exchange for other "privileges" such as an annual
annuity (treaty money), a once-off allocation of agricultural and other
tools and implements, and the right to hunt and fish on lands surrendered. The right of Treaty Indians to hunt and fish on surrendered
lands, in or out of season, without a provincial licence as required of
other hunters and fishers, continues to be a contentious issue between
Treaty Indians and other Canadian citizens, and frequently results in
litigation.

Aboriginal peoples first entered into treaty making with the
Crown under the understanding that they were continuing their well-

established tradition of agreements for "Peace and Friendship" based on mutual trust and respect. Today they seek full acknowledgement from the Crown of the betrayal of the spirit and intent of the treaties, and restoration of or restitution for lands and benefits promised but denied or taken away, as the basis for re-establishment of a relationship of mutual respect. Peoples who never signed treaties now seek new agreements as the way to regain some measure of control over land, resources, economy and government.

Contemporary treaties and land claim agreements (such as the James Bay and Northern Quebec Agreement of 1975, the Inuvialuit Final Agreement of 1984, and the Nunavut Land Claims Agreement of 1991) perpetuate the separation of Aboriginal peoples from others, by again setting aside relatively small and scattered parcels of land under exclusive Aboriginal control in exchange for surrender of title to all other lands specified in the agreement, plus cash settlements for past damages by non-Aboriginal users, compensation for future resource development profits surrendered, and rights to participate in decision making bodies responsible for renewable resource management. Again, these treaties have the multiple effect of separating Aboriginal signatories from other citizens, and of setting signatories apart from other Aboriginal peoples who have similar but unsettled claims, and from those who have been so long displaced from their traditional lands that they have little prospect of achieving a land claim agreement.

The historic and contemporary positioning of the "Original Peoples" in Canada as having particular and distinct rights, albeit rights not mutually agreed on or well understood by other Canadians (Morito, 1996), places them in conflict with the principle of equal rights for all citizens. Much of non-Aboriginal society repeatedly rejects the notion of the "special status" of Aboriginal people in Canada in terms of land "ownership," relationship to the federal government, or rights (to hunt and fish), despite the legal reality of that status. For some Canadians, this is simply ignorance of history and law. Others reject the premise that Canadian law singles out any group for special treatment, and call for repeal of all legislation, including the Treaties, Indian Act, and particular clauses in the Constitution and the Charter of Rights and Freedoms, which refer specifically to Aboriginal peoples and which confer particular rights on them not enjoyed by other Canadians.

Aboriginal communities are themselves divided internally. Aboriginal peoples in Canada live in geographic communities consisting of what Hansen (1985) calls "two realities." One reality is a "modern," industrializing, centralizing, increasingly hierarchically structured domain: the other is a "traditional" more-or-less subsistence-oriented domain. Most Aboriginal communities have their traditionalists, modernists and moderates: those who wish to renew the more traditional, land-based way of life, those who seek out and adopt new ways, and those who draw both from tradition and new ways. For many Aboriginal people, life-ways collide within the shared environment where the domains intersect. Indeed, traditionalists, modernists and moderates experience great difficulty in reaching any mutual understanding of what tradition is. "Real tradition exists, but the atmosphere which both sides (the non-traditionalist and traditionalist) promote is neither inherent to Mi'Kmaq culture nor a true measure of Mi'Kmaq tradition ... real tradition exists somewhere between the polarized interests" (Sark, 1996, 61-64). Furthermore, as Francis has documented in *The Imaginary Indian* (1992), non-Aboriginal society has taken on a role in defining who a "real" Indian, in large part by defining what Aboriginal tradition is. Non-Aboriginal society makes assumptions about what "real Indians" look like and how they should act, and presumes that stereotypes of past and localized traditions, such as the tepee, or the tomahawk, or feathered headdress, are traditions common to Aboriginal people across Canada. Recently though, the Supreme Court of Canada (in the *Sparrow* decision on the Aboriginal right to fish commercially) confronted this trend, by declaring that "tradition is not frozen in time": "tradition evolves."

Aboriginal traditions, such as the principles and practices of shared leadership and consensus decision making, which persist and are widespread (despite the authority bestowed on individual "chiefs" by the Indian Act), further inhibit the ability of Aboriginal leaders to speak with one voice on a given matter. Aboriginal society, in its many variations, is based on families and groupings of families into clans. Furthermore, contemporary settlements have brought together peoples who, in the past, did not live their lives year round in close association with each other, but who came together as the seasons dictated, for group activities, exchanges and ceremonies. Peoples from different traditions, cultures and in some cases languages, now find themselves living side by side in one residential settlement — a community of location rather than a community based on shared history or shared interests.

Families continue to dominate the life of contemporary Aboriginal communities, often being associated with particular activities in the community — elected government, formal schooling, hunting, healing, spiritual matters and ceremonies, and so on. The interests of people from different families and different groups may not coincide, making it difficult for members of these communities of location and residence to reach agreement on key issues, such as the direction and pace of change.

Nevertheless, the convention persists in Aboriginal society that spokespersons for a group may only speak to those matters already discussed and agreed upon by the group. Given the heterogeneity of even the smallest of contemporary Aboriginal communities, it is not surprising that Aboriginal leaders, from the most local to those who represent regional or national Aboriginal organizations, often state that they have no mandate to speak on behalf of their people, unless extensive consultations have already occurred. At the same time, a chief elected under the terms of the Indian Act can, and often will, take decisions with little formal consultation with community members.

Aboriginal society consists not of one people but of many. The laws and treaties of Canada have set Aboriginal people apart from other citizens in Canada, and have set groups of Aboriginal people apart from each other. Different processes and impacts of contact and colonization have been embraced and rejected differentially by individuals and groups. Persistence of traditional ways of coming to decisions constrains how a leader may properly act. They cannot, or may not, speak with one voice.

Aboriginal Perspectives on Relationships and Restructuring

The Royal Commission on Aboriginal Peoples divides the historic establishment of relationships between Aboriginal and non-Aboriginal society into four stages: first, what the Commission calls "separate worlds"; second, "contact and co-operation"; third, "displacement and assimilation"; and fourth and continuing, "negotiation and renewal" (RCAP, vol. 1, 1996, 36). Some scholars and commentators have criticized the Commission for depicting the first two stages as unrealistic "golden ages" of harmony and co-operation during which the above principles guided relationships. Others regard the Commission's depiction of the nature and substance of Aboriginal societies as grounded in relationships as an accurate depiction, and the descriptions and analysis of the destructive impacts of official policies as timely correctives.

The central, constructive theme of the Royal Commission, from which its analysis and its detailed recommendations all stem, is to use the understanding developed from stages one and two, and the impacts Aboriginal society experienced in stage three, to continue the work of stage four by restructuring relationships through negotiation and renewal.

Aboriginal society, the Commission suggests, was widely founded (and in some communities still is) on three principles: universal kinship, the primacy of individual conscience, and the endless creative power of the world. Barsh (1986), in a thoughtful discussion of North American political systems, invokes the old notion of "social compact" to convey the mutual understanding based on universal kinship of all life-forms, and of those life-forms which Western cultures regard as inanimate matter — air, fire, water, rock. Primacy of the individual is accompanied by and is consistent with a non-hierarchical society, where no decision making power is surrendered to representatives. No one has dominion over anyone else or anything else. The right of the individual is, nevertheless, counterbalanced by individual responsibility to the collective social unit, which is characteristically small, kin-based and close-knit. Collective decisions are constructed through slow and careful processes of consensus building.

The reciprocal relationships that bind this world are underpinned by defined responsibilities and mutual obligations. Life is focused on establishing and nurturing multiple relationships. Relationships are not regarded as static: circumstances change and relationships become unbalanced. They have to be renewed and reworked to restore harmony. Relationships are the foundation of the Aboriginal world — not structures or institutions or contracts. However, the core dilemmas which the Commission confronted are the same dilemmas which confound all attempts by Aboriginal peoples in Canada to engage non-Aboriginal society in dialogue directed to change. Three issues can be identified.

First: the relationship as presently constructed is neither equal nor respectful. It is undeniably unequal in terms of distribution of numbers of constituents and political and economic power, which are weighted heavily in favour of non-Aboriginal interests. In so far as they define Aboriginal rights in a positive manner, the historic and contemporary instruments defining the relationships, such as the treaties, land claims agreements, the Constitution, the Charter of Rights, and judgements of the Supreme Court, far from being promoted, have frequently been denied, ignored, or challenged by agencies of the state.

There has been little incentive for any level of government in Canada to commit to substantive restructuring of political, economic and social relationships, particularly when it may diminish non-Aboriginal access to land and resources in favour of Aboriginal access, and would require direct financial inputs. The recent refusal of the government of Newfoundland to consider forms of revenue sharing from the Voisey's Bay mining development with the Innu and Inuit or any reopening of the Innu land claim, is confirmation for Aboriginal people that government support for corporate profit prevails over principles and rights. Substantive changes, such as the implementation of legal decisions upholding Aboriginal rights and interests in crown lands and resources, or land settlements that fully address Aboriginal concerns, are perceived by the Canadian public to favour Aboriginal people over the rest of society, and carry political costs which few federal or provincial politicians are willing to incur. Politicians presume, probably correctly based on public response to shifts related to legal decisions pertaining to land and resources in British Columbia and New Brunswick, that the general public is reluctant to support restoration of Aboriginal rights and restitution for past wrongs.

Second, Aboriginal society is calling on non-Aboriginal society to comprehend, adopt and operate under Aboriginal principles: principles that have defined Aboriginal society. While these principles demand respect and apply widely within non-Aboriginal society, they are not the principles on which non-Aboriginal society is accustomed to base formal agreements. The formal basis of non-Aboriginal society, particularly in its interface with Aboriginal society, is less constructed around mutuality in relationships as it is arranged around what are essentially legal interpretations of social contracts and the agencies that carry them out. Dominant at the interface between the Aboriginal and non-Aboriginal domains are the treaties, the Indian Act, the Department of Indian and Northern Affairs, the Canadian courts and, more recently, the Constitution. The Commission's appeal for a joint endeavour is, therefore, bedevilled by the very different understandings and principles which the "partners" bring to the project, just as were the historic treaties described by Dickason.

Third, and problematic for the Royal Commission on Aboriginal Peoples as it is for virtually all Aboriginal organizations: if Aboriginal people use their own principles, processes, structures and vocabulary, they are not understood by the larger society and its key decision makers. Consequently, the Commission, in its pursuit of the grand agenda for change, invoked Aboriginal principles, but used not only the vocabulary but also the instruments of the dominant society when it proposed a new Royal Proclamation, renewed treaties, and new Acts of Parliament. (For a detailed and thoughtful discussion of why Aboriginal peoples have come to use a system of concepts and principles that has been instrumental in the destruction of their culture and identity, and why this can be regarded as a conciliatory act, see Morito, 1996.)

For this, the Commission has been widely criticized, particularly by Aboriginal people themselves. What, they ask, has the Royal Proclamation of 1763 done to ensure respect for Aboriginal nations? What real benefits or protection have the treaties conferred. The Indian Act has been an instrument of repression and disinheritance. Why should Aboriginal people seek new assurances from the government of Canada, in the form of new treaties and new Acts of the Canadian Parliament, when successive Canadian governments have not lived up to the spirit of the first Royal Proclamation, have not honoured existing treaties, have not acted on the insistent demands of Aboriginal people to reform and ultimately replace the Indian Act, and have not acted to affirm and promote Aboriginal rights as set out in the Constitution?

The internal contradictions of the Royal Commission on Aboriginal Peoples' approach to restructuring are embedded in Aboriginal adaptation and Aboriginal resistance, and in the nature of the long-standing relationships between the Aboriginal and non-Aboriginal domains in Canada. They are also embedded in the two major approaches or agendas pursued by Aboriginal leaders: the grand design for structural change, self-government and greater economic self-sufficiency through land settlements, upheld by new Canadian laws; and the immediate, localized and incremental approach to change.

RESTRUCTURING THROUGH INCREMENTAL CHANGE IN ABORIGINAL RIGHTS, POWERS, AND FUNCTIONS

Extraordinary political and institutional obstacles obstruct the ability of Aboriginal people to achieve the grand agenda that restructures relationships, namely: recognition of and support for Aboriginal rights and land title; full re-establishment of the right of self-government and recognition as a third order of government; accordance of wide government jurisdiction to Aboriginal nations; restoration of an adequate land base; and reallocation of land and resources to provide an economic base sufficient to support adequate financing of Aboriginal governments (RCAP 1996b, 7).

Despite, or perhaps because of the obstacles, gradual, piecemeal and incremental restructuring of the relationship between Aboriginal and non-Aboriginal society is an ongoing reality, and stems from a number of sources, including:

- recent rulings of the courts with respect to Aboriginal title to traditional lands and right of use of resources;
- exercise of new powers and/or use of resources resulting from negotiated settlement of various types of land rights issues;
- recent reaffirmation by the Government of Canada of the inherent right of self-government, within strict and specified limits;
- devolution of specific powers and functions from government agencies to Aboriginal groups as an outcome of joint negotiations;
- downloading and delegation of functions to Aboriginal groups by non-Aboriginal departments and agencies as part of upper-tier government policy to divest itself of program delivery; and
- insistence on the part of certain Aboriginal people that they will establish their own priorities and will manage specific aspects of community life of their choosing — that they will be selectively self-governing and self-managing.

The link between land and resource rights and greater Aboriginal self-government is clear. Rights and responsibilities with respect to land, peoples and resources are hollow and meaningless without powers, appropriate mechanisms, and financial and human resources to exercise the rights (Wolfe, 1995). These notions provide the filters with which to examine how substantive the incremental changes are, and what implications arise.

Rulings of the Courts with Respect to Title and Rights

Issues of Aboriginal title and rights to land and resources reach the courts through two rather different routes. Some Aboriginal peoples, notably the Nishga'a and the Gitsksan and Wet'suwet'en, have used litigation (as in the *Calder* and *Delgamuukw* cases) as a last resort in their struggle to assert unextinguished Aboriginal title to land threatened by external resource development, or when their claims have been rejected by government, or negotiations have failed to reach agreements they regard as satisfactory. The irony here is that Aboriginal peoples take to court the very institutions that are charged with the responsibility to protect their interests: institutions that have a fiduciary or trust relationship to uphold toward Aboriginal people. Concurrently, First Peoples who continue to exercise what they regard as their treaty or Aboriginal rights have regularly been taken to court by the same institutions for infractions of provincial or federal law (Saunders, 1992).

Several recent rulings of the courts, most notably *Sparrow v. R 1990*, *Delgamuukw v. R 1997* and *Paul 1997*, have affirmed Aboriginal title and rights to land and resources, and have implications which reach well beyond the individual cases. The Supreme Court decision on *Sparrow* speaks to the scope of Aboriginal rights protected by Section 35(1) of the Constitution Act of 1982. The Supreme Court decision on *Delgamuukw* affirms the existence of Aboriginal title in parts of Canada where no treaties have been signed. The New Brunswick upper court's decision on *Paul* acknowledges Aboriginal rights to use of the resources of Crown land in parts of Canada covered by historic treaty.

The *Sparrow* case required the Supreme Court of Canada, for the first time, to explore the scope of Section 35(1) of the Constitution Act of 1982, which gave protection to "existing Aboriginal and Treaty rights." The Court argued that an Aboriginal right exists and is therefore protected by Section 35(1), unless the Crown can show that it has been extinguished. The ruling imposes a significant burden on the Crown to justify legislation that infringes on rights protected by Section 35(1) of the Constitution Act. The fiduciary responsibility of the Crown to Aboriginal people must receive priority; the Crown must demonstrate a valid legislative objective; any infringement of Aboriginal rights must be minimized; Aboriginal groups must be consulted; and, in the case of expropriation, compensation must be offered.

The Court found that the Crown failed to prove that the Aboriginal right of Sparrow — a member of the Musqueam Band in British Columbia — to fish using a net longer than that permitted by his subsistence fishing licence, had been extinguished by virtue of the Fisheries Act. Moreover, said the Court, extinguishment may not be implied. There must be a "clear and plain intent to extinguish." The Court made reference to provincial law, saying that a provincial law, will not apply, to the extent that it interferes with an Aboriginal right,

unless there is a "compelling" reason for it to do so. A compelling justification would be the need to conserve and manage the resource. The
Court stated that laws and regulations must be drafted in such a way
that Aboriginal rights are "recognized and affirmed." Furthermore, the
Court stated that an existing Aboriginal right may be exercised in a
form that reflects a community's evolution and must be interpreted in
a large, generous and liberal way. Aboriginal rights are not "frozen in
time" (Usher 1991, Wagner, 1991, Isaac, 1993, Avio 1994). As Isaac
(1995, 329) notes: "recognition and affirmation (of Aboriginal rights)
requires sensitivity to and respect for Aboriginal peoples on behalf of
the government, courts, and indeed all Canadians."

After their case had been rejected in the British Columbia
Supreme Court and the Appeals Court had recognized their unextin-
guished non-exclusive Aboriginal rights, the Gitksan and Wet'suwet'en
peoples of northern British Columbia sought a declaration from the
Supreme Court of Canada affirming their ownership, jurisdiction
and Aboriginal rights over their traditional land. When eventually
the *Delgamuukw* case was heard before the Supreme Court, the
Court's decision was unequivocal and unanimous: the Gitksan and
Wet'suwet'en peoples have unextinguished title to traditional land.
The Supreme Court confirmed the title of Aboriginal peoples in British
Columbia to traditional land that the province has regarded as Crown
land and has managed as such.

The case is significant because most of the province of British
Columbia is without treaties. While the split Supreme Court judgement in the 1969 *Calder* case (in which the Nishga'a argued against the
province of B.C. for the existence of Aboriginal title) opened the way
for comprehensive claims settlement negotiations in other areas without treaties, it did not deter successive British Columbia governments
from refusing to engage in land claim negotiations. The *Delgamuukw*
judgement 28 years later has implications for the many Aboriginal
peoples in B.C. without treaty regarding the disposition and use of
Crown land in the province. It also has implications for other parts of
Canada where no treaties have yet been signed. It supports the position
of Aboriginal peoples that they may have unextinguished title to traditional land and associated resources, and places a heavy burden on the
provinces and federal government to deal in a timely fashion with
recognition of Aboriginal title, settlement of land claims, Aboriginal
input into land and resource use, share in resource revenues, and compensation. In March 1998, the governments of Canada and British
Columbia, and the B.C. First Nations agreed to a joint review of the

B.C. treaty process. Grand Chief Edward John commented that: "First Nations in this province require certainty just as much as business and government. The historic *Delgamuukw* decision gives us a unique opportunity to resolve how Aboriginal title and rights co-exist with the rights of others in British Columbia." In the 1997 *Paul* case, the Court of Queen's Bench of New Brunswick upheld a lower court decision that Aboriginals in New Brunswick have the right to harvest and sell trees taken off Crown land. The judge found that neither the Dunmer's Treaty of 1725 nor the Royal Proclamation of 1763 extinguished native rights in the land. On the contrary, he found that "Indians of New Brunswick do have land rights and that such are treaty rights," and ruled that Crown lands are reserved for Indians, and that "trees on Crown lands are Indian trees." A commercial enterprise may have a tree harvesting licence from the province, but treaty rights take priority. The potential implications of the case for provincial jurisdiction over Crown lands, and provincial management and licensing of the land and resources in New Brunswick and Nova Scotia are profound. The judgement casts doubt on the legitimacy of existing commercial licencing arrangements and raises the thorny issue of compensation to Aboriginal people in the two provinces for unrealized use and benefit. There is little doubt that the province of New Brunswick will appeal the judgement to the Supreme Court of Canada.

Aboriginal litigation over specific rights, as in *Sparrow, Paul* and many other cases, was aimed at getting recognition of those rights. Broader land rights cases, such as *Calder* and *Delgamuukw,* were intended to change government policy, to open up negotiations, and to set the stage for improved negotiated settlements (Saunders, 1992). Since 1984, the Supreme Court, in cases such as these, has been establishing the existence of Aboriginal rights to land and resources either as unextinguished rights or by virtue of treaty rights, and has been giving substance to the meaning of Aboriginal and treaty rights as mentioned in the Constitution Act. Aboriginal interests in land and resources can no longer be ignored. However, legal judgements do not deal with the implications emanating from the decisions; implications that still have to be dealt with through negotiation or through legislation.

Exercise of Powers and Use of Resources
through Land Rights and Compensation Settlements

In those areas where no formal land treaties have been signed, such as British Columbia and Labrador, Aboriginal people continue to seek formal recognition of their title to their traditional land and recognition of their right to exercise powers of government over land, peoples and resources. The British Columbia, Newfoundland and New Brunswick governments have proved reluctant to enter into negotiations on treaty issues. Court decisions are now propelling these governments to the negotiating table.

Peoples who have completed contemporary land treaties, like the James Bay Cree and Inuit of northern Quebec, the Inuvialuit in the northwestern Northwest Territories (NWT), the Inuit of Nunavut in the eastern NWT and, most recently, the Yukon Indians, have gained title to part (albeit a small part) of their traditional land base and formal representation on land and resource management boards making decisions on use and development on traditional land to which they do not have full title. They have also received a financial package in compensation for land and resources which have not passed into Aboriginal title, for benefits which they did not receive, and for damages created by the activities of others.

Through terms of comprehensive claims settlements, Aboriginal groups across large areas of the North are now positioned to make decisions on land and resource development proposals with respect to land to which they have full title. As members of mandatory management boards, they participate in land and resource management decisions in those parts of the territories and provinces covered by the agreement but not by Aboriginal title. However, the advisory, review and decision making system that is emerging is very cumbersome, with overlapping jurisdictions and power struggles within and between emerging authorities.

Many peoples are using the financial package they received from conclusion of a land claim to support their own institutions of government and service delivery. This affords local and regional Aboriginal agencies a degree of autonomy in setting policy and implementing programs not enjoyed elsewhere. Again though, these agencies are in serious financial difficulties as the needs of the youthful and rapidly growing remote communities exceed available financial resources.

Many groups have used part of the financial package from settlement of a comprehensive land claim or from revenue sharing from development of land and resources in which they have a legal interest or have legal title to set up their own investment and lending agencies to stimulate an array of individual and community-based economic development initiatives. Where they command either the financial or material resource base, Aboriginal groups are setting up business corporations and banking and lending systems, are seeking non-Aboriginal venture capital, and are engaging in joint businesses with non-Aboriginal partners. Several, such as the Meadow Lake Tribal Council in Saskatchewan, have carefully positioned their business ventures to meet an array of social, political and economic goals (Anderson and Bone, 1995).

Aboriginal people have argued strenuously that the contemporary treaties must include provisions for establishing effective instruments of Aboriginal government. For two decades, the federal government refused to include any reference to self-government within the terms of a land claim settlement. Because they have the legal status of a treaty, land claims settlements automatically gained constitutional protection under section 35(1) of the Constitution Act, 1982. Inclusion of self-government provisions would extend that protection to Aboriginal governments: something that the federal government was not then ready to do. While recent federal policy changes have removed this restriction, the new policy places specific limits on the range of Aboriginal government authority.

Reaffirmation by the Government of Canada of the Inherent Right to Self-Government within Specified Limits

For decades if not centuries, Aboriginal peoples have been arguing that they have an inherent and unextinguished right to self-government, and have sought ways to secure legal or legislative recognition of that right. With little fanfare and as yet no additional legislation, the federal government has reaffirmed the inherent right to self-government as an existing Aboriginal right under section 35(1) of the Constitution Act, 1982. The government acknowledges that: "the inherent right may be enforceable through the courts, and that there may be different views on the nature, scope and content of that right" (Minister of Indian Affairs and Northern Development, 1995, 3).

The federal government has, therefore, set out its view of the nature and scope of the Aboriginal right to self-government. In so doing, it has set strict limits on Aboriginal jurisdiction. The government states that the scope of Aboriginal jurisdiction or authority extends only to matters that are internal to the group, to matters integral to its distinct Aboriginal culture, and matters essential to its operation as a government. While the scope of Aboriginal authority is limited, matters open for negotiation include administration and enforcement of Aboriginal laws; property rights including succession and estates; adoption and child welfare; membership; and policing (Minister of Indian Affairs and Northern Development, 195, 5-6). The policy statement also makes it clear that the federal government intends to retain primary law-making authority across several matters in which Aboriginal groups have a significant interest: gaming, fisheries co-management, administration of justice issues, labour and training, and all matters related to Canadian sovereignty and the national interest.

Within these constraints, and they are considerable, the federal government has been quietly focusing on negotiations with individual First Nations to develop arrangements for greater self-government which are tailored to particular circumstances. This is a departure, in rhetoric if not in substance, from previous positions of the federal government, which had clung to the model of limited municipal-style Aboriginal governments with specified and delegated powers, and the corollary that the one model should fit all. Frameworks are in place through which First Nations and the federal government can negotiate agreements on greater self-government within the terms of existing treaties. Further, the way is now open for Aboriginal government to be included within the Comprehensive Claims Process.

Much as these steps go some way toward addressing the Aboriginal agenda for self-government, they are limited. Absence of umbrella legislation, many Aboriginal leaders argue, continues to leave their governments vulnerable to having their authority revoked or further limited by the federal government. The scope of Aboriginal jurisdiction is not set by Aboriginal people themselves, or even through negotiation, but by federal fiat. On the other hand, the negotiating framework does provide a flexible vehicle for greater Aboriginal self-government tailored to specific needs. But, as with all such negotiated settlements, though, the process of negotiation is very slow. Furthermore, there is a tendency on the part of federal negotiators to squeeze Aboriginal governments into a particular set of jurisdictions, which seem logical to the external observer. That being said, many Aboriginal nations are aware that they may not have the capacity to exercise effectively those powers that they do take on; concerns also expressed by other levels of government.

While the existing framework for Aboriginal government does not meet the legislative agenda recommended by the Commission (Table 7, item 2), the federal government's 1998 Agenda for Action calls for the development, jointly with Aboriginal peoples, of a National Recognition Instrument, one component of which would involve legislation to recognize First Nations governments (Minister of Indian Affairs and Northern Development, 1998, 5). The 1998 proposal also includes a Governance Transition Centre which would operate at arms length from government and support capacity building to design and operate Aboriginal institutions of governance.

Devolution of Powers

Some Aboriginal peoples are successfully negotiating new relationships with other levels of government and with other partners, in large part because their interests align with those of the non-Aboriginal domain, because the changes do not set significant precedents, or because the demands are deemed to pose no major threat to the overall status quo.

The project to dismantle the machinery of the Department of Indian Affairs in Manitoba, which is proceeding very slowly, is one such example; the establishment of the Inuit majority government of Nunavut, which is scheduled to come into effect on April 1, 1999 is, arguably, another; the Community Negotiations program of the Department of Indian Affairs (formerly known as the Self-Government Negotiations) is a third.

For example, provisions of the Community Negotiations program substantially expand the range of powers and functions that band councils may exercise beyond the limitations set by the Indian Act, and offers optional special federal legislation to give substance and security to the changes. The program is designed to accommodate expanded Indian government within the existing constitutional framework, and does not alter the division of powers between governments (Department of Indian Affairs and Northern Development, 1988).

While the Indian Act has not been repealed or replaced, changes to the Act over the past decade allow Indian band councils to set and administer their own membership code and increase councils' power to control residency on reserves. Amendments in 1988 provided bands with expanded financial powers, including the right to levy property taxes and to control development on reserves.

These examples entail shifts of authority from one government to another. They are adapted to particular regional circumstances and open the way for fine-tuning at the local, community level. But each Aboriginal government has to negotiate within frameworks determined by another level of government, and pre-set limits are placed on the range of powers they can assume and functions they may take on. Furthermore, even with allowing the extension of powers of taxation to some Aboriginal governments, none can command sufficient of their own resources to be self-sufficient. Also, the new mechanisms of government appear to be little different from those that they replaced, and are no less bureaucratic.

Again, success of these shifts over the long term is predicated in part on the willingness of the federal government to maintain or increase funding levels, and in part on the capacity of the Aboriginal governments and agencies to run themselves and, over the longer term, to redesign and streamline their governments. Differences between non-Aboriginal and Aboriginal expectations for government, and tensions between the Aboriginal nation or tribal council and the Aboriginal community or band will also continue to limit the effectiveness of Aboriginal governments.

DOWNLOADING OF PROGRAMS
AND DELEGATION OF FUNCTIONS

Another source of incremental change in Aboriginal government is a consequence of bureaucratic downloading. By this I mean the numerous incremental changes initiated by governments to streamline departments and service delivery agencies. As they respond to Canada-wide agendas for restructuring, downsizing, and greater efficiency, government departments and non-Aboriginal service delivery agencies seek out approaches that worked for one people, often initiated by an Aboriginal nation or community, and develop "models" which they then impose on other communities or nations. Bureaucratic principles of simplicity, uniformity and conformity override the Aboriginal reality of cultural diversity.

Some observers suggest that there is a tendency for bureaucracies to devolve most readily those matters which incur greatest costs, or which they find particularly difficult to deal with, with potentially very negative consequences for the communities taking on the new service delivery responsibilities (Quarles van Ufford, 1988). Furthermore, responsibility is not matched by increased power and adequate funds. As Culhane-Speck noted in the context of the Health Transfer Program: "First Nations leaders are offered the doubtful pleasure of being held responsible for health and health care by their communities, while remaining accountable to and dependent upon the federal government" (Culhane-Speck, 1989, 205). Alternative Funding Arrangements and, more recently, Financial Transfer Agreements are agreements between the Government of Canada and First Nations through which a block of funding is transferred to a First Nation for use across a range of needs such as education, housing, water and sewerage systems, capital projects and other priorities, typically for a period of five years. This approach to funding replaces annual allotments for federally defined and highly specific programs, and enables a First Nation signatory to set priorities and tailor programs to meet community-identified priorities. Financial Transfer Agreements are essentially performance contracts designed to ensure a set quality and level of service is provided to members of First Nations' communities through responsibilities delegated to that Nation's government.

What was at first a "trickle-down" has become a cascade as Aboriginal nations have themselves demanded more involvement in, and responsibility for, delivery of key services, and both federal and provincial departments and ministries have downloaded functions. Many communities simply do not have sufficiently trained and formally educated members to carry out the numerous and demanding tasks involved in transfer and related programs. As a result, they struggle, and either fail to run well-managed programs, or recruit staff from outside the community and again run the risk of losing control of programs or projects to outsiders. Occurring together and impacting on each small Aboriginal community, the convergence of bureaucratic offloading and Aboriginal demand for a stronger voice in decision making may have the counterproductive effect of overwhelming or crippling them — what I call the "cascade and drowning" effect (Wolfe, 1994). Aboriginal people suggest that all that is really happening is that "we are now expected to administer our own misery."

Aboriginal Self-Government and Self-Management

Across Canada, peoples like the Nishnawbe-Aski Nation in northwestern Ontario (Nothing and Wolfe, 1993), the Walpole Island First Nation (Cassidy and Bish 1989), or the Meadow Lake Tribal Council (Andersen and Bone, 1995) continue the struggle to pursue their own agendas, and establish their own agencies to deal with community priorities. High on many community agendas are matters such as programs involving physical, sexual and substance abuse; child welfare

and child care; appropriate community-directed education and training; new approaches to community policing and community justice,
including community sentencing circles; and environmental and
resource development grounded in Aboriginal understanding of wise
use and management. Healing, cultural preservation and revitalization,
and exercise of greater decision making control over all matters deemed
critical to community survival and "thrival" form the core of Aboriginal
self-government and self-management.

Initiatives taken by tribal councils and other supra-local community entities reflect the gradual acceptance on the part of Aboriginal
peoples that the community or band level is simply too small an entity
to meet the full range of needs, and that, difficult as it is, greater self-
government may be more rapidly and effectively achieved through
co-operation at the level of the Aboriginal nation.

Communities are pioneering models and processes that take multiple objectives into account (Andersen, 1995). Changes such as these
reflect the growing capacity of some communities to, selectively, make
their own decisions and manage their own affairs.

RESTRUCTURING IMPLICATIONS FOR ABORIGINAL AND NON-ABORIGINAL SOCIETIES

All of these initiatives demonstrate the tenacity of Aboriginal peoples in
seeking out opportunities to address needs as they understand them,
and, as Cassidy and Bish (1989) put so well, to express the meaning of
Aboriginal government in practice. Consequently, a complex mosaic is
emerging wherein some Aboriginal communities and nations have
tightened their security of title to land; or expanded their land and
resource base; or increased their role in decision making over jointly
administered lands and resources; or improved their share of benefits to
be derived from utilization of resources; or significantly broadened
their powers and functions of government. Others have gained few of
these improvements.

A small but increasing number of contemporary Aboriginal governments exercise policy, program and project authority over a range of
functions far greater than that exercised by even the largest lower-tier
municipal governments. These governments are a sometimes highly
functional and oftentimes uneasy mix of traditional and non-tradition-
al elements. The emergent governments are tending to mirror the organizations that previously administered them, and with which they have

to negotiate change. In order to meet external expectations and interface with non-Aboriginal government agencies, they are drawn into an increasingly bureaucratic rather than less bureaucratic system. Tensions are now apparent between the bureaucratic structures and processes of contemporary Aboriginal governments and the consensus decision making principles, interpersonal relationships and informality of community tradition.

Important as is the determination of Aboriginal people to improve their situation, effectiveness is not only contingent on the extent to which they exert the authority they have grasped, use the powers which have been devolved to them, or manage the functions which have been downloaded. It is also contingent on the extent to which they can command appropriate financial and human resources. It is also contingent on the willingness, or refusal, of other governments, the Canadian public, and corporate interests to accept the redefinition of Aboriginal rights that is occurring through litigation, and to support reaffirmation of those rights through legislation.

With a few notable exceptions, Canada's responses continue to be consistent with its firmly established policy of support and protection for what it regards as the larger public interest in the frequent situations when this collides with an Aboriginal interest as continues to occur on all of Canada's development and resource frontiers, be they with respect to mining, hydroelectric development, forestry, commercial or sports fishery, or the establishment of parks. This is coupled with continued state intervention in Aboriginal life. Canada's responses, again with a few notable exceptions, are consistent with its unwillingness or inability to hear and to heed what Aboriginal people want. National reluctance to confront and respond positively to an Aboriginal agenda that insists that special and collective rights of the country's Indigenous peoples must be acknowledged within Canadian society — also that these rights are consistent with, and can contribute to, the flourishing of a liberal and democratic society.

Aboriginal people insist they are "citizens different," and have legal, constitutional and historical evidence, and moral argument, to support their claim. Acceptance of this by non-Aboriginal Canada is the foundation stone for reconciliation and renewed relationships. Canada's understanding of a liberal democracy in which all people are equal and treated equally will continue to be challenged by an Aboriginal concept of democracy which not only tolerates but supports political and economic institutions that are consciously grounded in distinctions between peoples.

Such substantive restructuring as has occurred can be attributed to one piece of legislation, the Canadian Constitution Act, 1982, and several pieces of litigation, including the post-1984 favourable rulings of the Supreme Court of Canada on Aboriginal rights and title. Further restructuring of relationships has to confront and redress the complex set of issues surrounding Aboriginal rights, which Canada and Canadians have ignored or deliberately deferred. Decisions of the courts are now requiring that these rights be given due attention. What continues to be missing, though, is the sustained, constructive and willing engagement of non-Aboriginal Canadian society to implement the vision of a joint and mutually respectful project of reconciliation, restructuring and reconstruction.

DEDICATION

This chapter is dedicated to the memory of Dr. H.C. "Nugget" Coombs, beloved mentor and friend, whose book *Kulinma: Listening to Aborigines* (1978) provides the inspiration for the title of this chapter, and reminds me constantly of how poorly we all listen and heed. Nugget died on October 29, 1997, at the age of 91, and was eulogized across Australia as "a very great Australian, perhaps the greatest of all." During his more than 30 years as a senior bureaucrat, and serving under seven different Prime Ministers, he was Director of Rationing in Australia during World War II, Director of Postwar Reconstruction and, for nearly 20 years, Governor of the Commonwealth Bank of Australia and the Reserve Bank. After his retirement as Governor of the Bank, he served as Chair of the Australian Council for the Arts, first full-time Chancellor of the Australian National University, President of the Australian Conservation Foundation, and first Chair of the Australian Council for Aboriginal Affairs. For the last 30 years of his life, Nugget Coombs was an influential and highly respected social, economic and environmental critic and advocate, who "listened to Aborigines" and wrote frankly and persuasively about what he heard. Throughout his life, he was an enduring positive force in Australia. He touched the lives of all who knew him and is sorely missed.

REFERENCES

Anderson, R. (1995), "The Business Economy of the First Nations in Saskatchewan: A Contingency Perspective," *Canadian Journal of Native Studies*, vol. 15, no. 2, 309-46.

Anderson, R., and R. Bone (1995), "First Nations' Economic Development: A Contingency Perspective," *Canadian Geographer*, vol. 39, no. 2, 120-30.

Avio, K.L. (1994), "Aboriginal Property Rights in Canada: A Contractarian Interpretation of *R. v. Sparrow*," *Canadian Public Policy*, vol. 20, no. 4, 415-29.

Barsh, R.L. (1986), "The Nature and Spirit of North American Political Systems," *American Indian Quarterly*, vol. 10, no. 3, 181-98.

Beckett, J. (1988), "Aboriginality, Citizenship and the Nation State," *Social Analysis*, vol. 24 (special issue on "Aborigines and the State in Australia," J. Beckett, ed.), 3-18.

Berger, T. (1991), *A Long and Terrible Shadow: White Values, Native Rights in the Americas, 1492-1992* (Toronto: Douglas and McIntyre).

Boldt, M. (1981), "Social Correlates of Nationalism: A Study of Native Indian Leaders in a Canadian Internal Colony," *Comparative Political Studies*, vol. 14, no. 2, 205-31.

Cardinal, H. (1969), *The Unjust Society: The Tragedy of Canada's Indians* (Edmonton: Hurtig Publications).

Cassidy, F., and R. Bish (1989), *Indian Government: Its Meaning in Practice* (Lantzville, B.C. and Halifax: Oolichan Books and the Institute for Public Policy).

Coates, K., and J. Powell (1989), *The Modern North: People, Politics and the Rejection of Colonialism* (Toronto: James Lorimer).

Culhane-Speck, D. (1989), "The Indian Health Transfer Policy: A Step in the Right Direction or Revenge of the Hidden Agenda," *Native Studies Review*, vol. 5, no. 1, 187-214.

Francis, D. (1992), *The Imaginary Indian: The Image of the Indian in Canadian Culture* (Vancouver: Arsenal Pulp Press).

Frideres, J.S. (1988), *Native Peoples in Canada: Contemporary Conflicts*, 2nd edn. (Scarborough, Ont.: Prentice-Hall).

Hansen, B. (1985), *Dual Realities — Dual Strategies* (Saskatoon, Saskatchewan: Bill Hansen).

Hawthorne, H., *et al.* (1967), *The Survey of Contemporary Indians of Canada*, vols. 1, 2 (Ottawa: Department of Indian and Northern Affairs).

Imai, S., *et al.* (1993), *Aboriginal Law Handbook* (Scarborough, Ont.: Carswell).

Isaac, T. (1993), "Balancing Rights: The Supreme Court of Canada,

R. v. Sparrow, and the Future of Aboriginal Rights," *Canadian Journal of Native Studies*, vol. 12, no. 2, 199-219.

Isaac, T. (1995), *Aboriginal Law: Cases, Materials and Commentary* (Saskatoon, Sask.: Purich Press).

Knight, D.B. (1998), "Canada and its Political Fault-lines: Reconstitution or Disintegration," in *Tension Areas of the World*, D.G. Bennett, ed. (Dubuque, IA: Kendall Hunt), 207-27.

Miller, J. (1989), *Skyscrapers Hide the Heavens* (Toronto: University of Toronto Press).

Minister of Indian Affairs and Northern Development (1995), *Aboriginal Self-Government: The Government of Canada's Approach to the Implementation of the Inherent Right and the Negotiation of Aboriginal Self-Government*, Federal Policy Guide (Ottawa: Minister of Public Works and Government Services Canada).

———— (1997), *Gathering Strength — Canada's Aboriginal Action Plan* (Ottawa: Minister of Public Works and Government Services Canada).

———— (1998), *Agenda for Action with First Nations* (Ottawa: Minister of Public Works and Government Services Canada).

Morito, B. (1996), "Aboriginal Right: A Conciliatory Concept," *Journal of Applied Philosophy*, vol. 13, no. 2, 123-39.

Nothing, B., and J. Wolfe (1993), "Reintegrating People, Land and Government: The Nishnawbe-Aski Nations in Northern Ontario," in *Indigenous Land Rights in Commonwealth Countries: Dispossession, Negotiation and Community Action*, G. Cant, *et al.* (Christchurch, NZ: Department of Geography, University of Canterbury and Ngai Tahu Maori Trust Board), 121-31.

Penner, K. (1983), *Indian Self-Government in Canada: Report of the Special All-party Committee* [Penner Report] (Ottawa: Ministry of Supply and Services Canada).

Perkson, G. (1993), "Plastic Words," discussed on "Ideas," Toronto: Canadian Broadcasting Corporation.

Quarles van Ufford, P. (1988), "The Hidden Crisis in Development: Development Bureaucracies in Between Intentions and Outcomes," in *The Hidden Crisis in Development: Development Bureaucracies*, P. Quarles van Ufford, *et al.*, eds. (Amsterdam: UN University of Tokyo and Free University), 9-38.

Rowse, T. (1992), *Remote Possibilities: The Aboriginal Domain and the Administrative Imagination* (Darwin: Australian National University, North Australia Research Unit).

Royal Commission on Aboriginal Peoples (1996), *Report of the Royal Commission on Aboriginal Peoples*, vol. 1: *Looking Forward: Looking Back*; vol. 2: *Restructuring the Relationship*; vol. 3: *Gathering Strength*; vol. 4: *Perspectives and Realities*; vol. 5: *Renewal: A Twenty-Year Commitment* (Ottawa: Ministry of Supply and Services Canada).

———— (1996a), *People to People: Nation to Nation — Highlights of the Report's Findings and Conclusions* (Ottawa: Ministry of Supply and Services Canada).

———— (1996b), *Guide to the Principal Findings and Recommendations of the Final Report of the Royal Commission on Aboriginal Peoples* (Ottawa: Ministry of Supply and Services Canada).

Sark, C. (1996), "Identity, Community and Development: The Experience of the Lennox Island First Nation," M.Sc. Major Research Project, University School of Rural Planning and Development, University of Guelph.

Saunders, D. (1992), "Getting Back to Rights," in *Aboriginal Title in British Columbia: Delgamuukw v. The Queen*, F. Cassidy, ed. (Lantzville, B.C: Oolichan Books and the Institute for Research on Public Policy), 261-87.

Satzewich, V., and T. Wotherspoon (1993), *First Nations: Race, Class and Gender Relations* (Scarborough, Ont.: Nelson).

Stokes, E. (1992), "The Treaty of Waitangi and the Waitangi Tribunal: Maori Claims in New Zealand," *Applied Geography*, vol. 12, no. 2, 176-91.

Trigger, B. (1985), *Natives and Newcomers: Canada's Heroic Age Reconsidered* (Montreal: McGill-Queen's University Press).

Usher, P. (1991), "Some Implications of the Sparrow Judgement for Resource Conservation and Management," *Alternatives*, vol. 13, no. 2, 20-21.

Wagner, M.W. (1991), "Footsteps Along the Road: Indian Land Claims and Access to Natural Resources," *Alternatives*, vol. 18, no. 2, 23-27.

Watkins, M. (1972), *The Dene Nation: A Colony Within* (Toronto: University of Toronto Press).

Wolfe, J. (1992), "Changing the Pattern of Aboriginal Self-Government in Canada," in *Contemporary Rural Systems in Transition*, I.R. Bowler, C.R. Bryant, and M.D. Nellis, eds., vol. 2, *Economy and Society* (Oxford: CAB International), 294-306.

Wolfe, J. (1994), *Sustaining Aboriginal Community Development Planning: Case Studies of Non-Governmental Approaches* (Darwin: Australian National University, North Australia Research Unit, Discussion Paper no. 22).

———— (1994), "First Nations' Strategies for Reintegrating People, Land, Resources and Government," in *Public Issues: A Geographical Perspective*, J. Andrey, and J.G. Nelson, eds. (Waterloo: University of Waterloo, Department of Geography Publication Series, no. 41), 239-70.

———— (1995), "First Nations' Sovereignty and Land Claims," in *Resource and Environmental Management in Canada: Addressing Conflict and Uncertainty*, B. Mitchell, ed. (Don Mills, Ont.: Oxford University Press), 55-79.

INDEX

(Indigenous peoples *cont'd*)
Oka, 113, 125
Red Paper, 124-25
reserves, 113-14
Royal Commission on
Aboriginal Peoples, 124-33,
143-46, 153
self-government, 18, 125,
129-30, 132, 134, 147,
152-54, 156-57
White Paper, Indians' status,
118, 124, 125
Industrial parks, 86-87
Industrialization, 2, 3
Inflation, 42-43
Insecurity, job, 68-70, 74
International Monetary Fund, 52
International trade, 35

J-K
Joseph, Alun E., xi-xii, 1, 17, 18,
123
Kitchener-Waterloo, 83, 90, 96, 101
Knight, David B., xi, 1, 123

L
Labour markets, 43, 90
Labrador, 150
Land use, 45
Lange, David, 38
Law, see
Calder case, 147, 149-150
Delgamuukw case, 134,
147-150
Indian Act, 114, 140, 141, 142,
145, 154
international law, 106, 119
natural law, 18, 105, 118
Paul case, 148, 150
Sparrow case, 134, 142, 148
Leach, Belinda, xii, 16-17, 20, 83
Lithuania, 3
Local, 14, 17

Localization, 53-54
Los Angeles, 89

M
Manitoba, 65
Manufacturing, 41, 59, 89-90; and
Canada Packers, 90-91, 96-97
just-in-time, 59
outsourcing, 16
lay-offs, 70, 72, 90-99
plant closure, 17, 87, 90-91,
96-97
Westinghouse, 87, 90-91,
95-96, 98
Marginalization, 9
Maritimes, 105
Market liberalization, 41
Market process, 36
Marketing boards, 43-45
Mennonite, 14
Mercredi, Ovide, 132
Mississauga, 98
Moderation, 31
Modernization, 2, 3
Montreal, 61
Moran, Warren, xiii, 16, 17, 18, 20,
33, 123
Mount Forest, 86-87, 90-91, 96, 98

N
Nationalism, 4
New Zealand, 2, 4, 6, 9-16, 18, 20,
33-54, 123; and
New Zealand experiment, 6,
33-34, 38
Pakeha, 12
(see also Aboriginal People,
Government, Ideology, Law)
New Brunswick, 89, 145, 148, 150
Newfoundland, 65, 145
North American Free Trade
Agreement, 91
Northland, 12